The

FACES

behind the pages that

INSPIRE

The
FACES

behind the pages that

INSPIRE

UNTOLD STORIES ABOUT PEOPLE
WHO EMPOWER US EVERY DAY

BOOK 3
in the *A Victim No More* Series

LORI REKOWSKI
and
FRIENDS

Internet addresses given in this book were
accurate at the time it went to press.

Author Lori Rekowski is available as a speaker and consultant.
Please visit www.facesbehindthepagesthatinspire.com for her schedule of
appearances.

Cover and Interior design by Frame25 Productions
www.frame25productions.com
Cover art © ra2 studio c/o Shutterstock.com (computer and hand image)
Yuri Arcurs c/o Shutterstock.com (faces montage)

Library of Congress Cataloging-in-Publication Data
available upon request

ISBN: 978-1482598971

Rekowski, Lori, 1962-
The Faces Behind the Pages That Inspire/Lori Rekowski & Friends
Includes bibliographical references.

Contents

Dedication

It takes one person to believe in you. One person who won't give up on you. And you may never know exactly how much that faith affects the one that you may be unconsciously inspiring. That person, for me, is the person that I dedicate this book to: Dr. Walid Mikhail. Thank you for your eternal faith in the warrior spirit that always was there, deep within me. And a sincere expression of my deep gratitude goes out to you, right here and right now, for never buying into my "story" of playing small. You never bought into my "poor-me tale of a tragedy." Instead, you compassionately held the space for me to grow into the person that you knew I could be.

There is no other person on this planet that I would trust more to watch out for my highest good when it comes to my health, than you . . . except for myself, now. I honor you more than you will ever know—for that selfless belief in me, my friend. Especially when I was deep in the middle of the pain and confusion of my brain injury recovery, I will never forget when you asked me, "When are you going to get your next book out?" You taught me, by example, that it is possible to live free of judgment. Well, here you go . . . this one's for you! And, you thought that I'd forgotten?

Namaste'.

Lori Rekowski

How difficult the task to quench the fire and the pride of private ambition, and to sacrifice ourselves and all our hopes and expectations to the public weal! How few have souls capable of so noble an undertaking! How often are the laurels worn by those who have had no share in earning them! But there is a future recompense of reward, to which the upright man looks, and which he will most assuredly obtain, provided he perseveres unto the end.

—Abigail Adams

Preface

In this second volume of *The Faces Behind the Pages that Inspire,* I am taking the message about leaving the victim mindset one step further. For this particular edition of the A Victim No More series, I carefully chose Facebook fan page administrators who not only overcame the victim consciousness, they—like our first set of authors—have moved beyond the personal responsibility that comes with freeing yourself from that old paradigm of pain-filled dramas. They plunged forward, with faith in humanity, into the next stage that comes with this freedom. They began, like me, to realize that they are all connected to one another on many levels. Scientists have now proved beyond a shadow of a doubt that the energy field is linked to our DNA structures.

Thanks to the generosity of some very special people whom you are about to meet, many have found the safe "space" for expressing their social outrage at what is happening to us all on this planet right now. Better yet? They are willing to open their eyes and take action to join these changemakers in doing something about the various travesties that so many of us throughout the world agree need to be put to a stop. There is a call for transformation in nearly every country in the world right now. Some of those suffering are speaking up, and some still suffer silently. Yet there is no doubt that there is unrest among global citizens.

> *Every action and decision we take – or don't – ripples into the future. For the first time we have the capability, the technology, and the knowledge to direct these ripples.*
> — Jacque Fresco

Who are these driving forces behind the scenes who find themselves dedicated, day in and day out—passionate about their causes—to serving and encouraging their *followers* tirelessly? Now you can meet them, here in the pages of this remarkable book.

This book will reveal their very personal stories of victim-to-victor–to-advocates. These heartwarming and inspiring life stories will take you on a journey of hope, wonder, fascination, and encouragement.

We are all works in progress; every single one of us is, until the day that we leave this planet. And, as for me? I am learning to balance my passions with a healthy dose of practicality. Want to join me?

"True alignment with our spiritual nature will eventually evoke a sense of social responsibility."

-Bernard Alvarez

facebook.com/FacesBehindThePages

Introduction

After my book *A Victim No More, How to Break Free from Self-Judgment* (most recently subtitled "How to Stop Being Taken Advantage Of") was published by Hampton Roads Publishing, I cannot begin to count the number of people who said, "I should write a book about my life. I have been through so many horrible things," or a comment of that ilk.

And I would always answer, "Well, this isn't a book about all the awful things that I went through, it's a book about how I left those old stories behind." It's a book about healing tools and principles that you can apply to change your life forever. It's about how to stop giving your power away to someone or something else, and to learn to take that power back without shame, blame, or guilt still running rampant and controlling your thought process. Those same painful, indoctrinated beliefs and habitual practices, I would add, work well to undermine any freedom of choice that you would make to be an empowered person who loves and respects yourself. Worse yet? Add a little dose of fear-based judgment, and you have the perfect mix of disempowerment.

Self-judgment is the telltale sign—or "tattoo," if I may—of someone who has left his or her self-worth in the past (if they ever had any) and feels the need to win others' constant approval, often by striving to be a perfectionist and people pleaser. And, whether any of us want to admit it or not, we automatically project judgment onto others when we habitually do it to ourselves.

The victim mindset is often a perpetual wheel of pain, drama, and misery. Yet, most of the population is stuck in it. We've allowed ourselves to become victims of our society. Don't believe me? Turn on the evening news, or hop online and take a peek at what's happening in our world today. If you haven't seen a story on rioting or peaceful demonstrations gone awry; shootings in the workplace, church, or school; millions of homes being foreclosed on, and so on, then you've been burying your head in the sand. Or worse: You don't care or you feel that you can't do anything about it. The authors in this book think much differently. They are well aware of the tragic events occurring on this planet and they are doing something about it. They are educating people on what is happening by using facts and examples to show *why it is all happening.*

As for my own personal struggles? I will be the first to admit that I had left almost all of those "stories" out of the original edition of *A Victim No More,* Instead, I focused only on the healing tools that I had learned. In fact, I just listed the difficulties that I had been through and summarized my entire life in six short pages. Frankly, the only reason that I added my personal story to the book, as it now reads, was that the very first review I received said it was a great book, but it would be far more powerful if I had shared some of my personal struggles so that the readers could relate more personally to me and, therefore, feel more connected and hopeful. And since my deep passion is to reach my hand out to others and assist them out of the type of living hell that I once resided in, I complied and shared some of the painful events that I lived through.

When I first read that review, I thought "darn it!" I KNEW that this was going to happen." My intuition had already told me that I'd have to reveal more details about events that caused the trauma. And so, the painful journey began. I revisited memories of my childhood and those leading to the present moment. I had to relive and share the traumatic events that had occurred while I was still living in the thick of the victim mindset. It wasn't fun. However, I will share this: It ended up being an important part of my own personal healing journey.

Mindfulness techniques assisted me in not allowing some of the really painful memories to disturb my present peace of mind. I have always discovered that when I am willing to do something for the highest good of all—and reach out and work on behalf of others—then in the end what I give always comes back a thousand fold, one way or another. This case was no different.

For those of us who are willing to do this work, when we choose to go public, we often find that it's never easy to divulge our drama-filled stories between the covers of a book. We often face ridicule from our families, and sometimes old friends and co-workers. When you leave the old tribal mentality behind, not everyone is so thrilled when you happen to rock his or her boat. Think about it. If you've stepped away and out of that life, then they might have to look at theirs. Follow me?

Simply put, it takes a lot of courage. And so why do we do it? For the purpose of this book, I've asked my co-authors to share their stories so that their Facebook subscribers, and you the readers, can have real-life examples of who these amazing Facebook page administrators are, why they do what they do, and how far they've come. And in the process, we all learn about the experiences that impassioned them to want to help others in the first place.

What is it that makes these pages so real, so powerful, thought-provoking, and authentic? These are stories of triumph, not tragedy. These are real-life people working behind the scenes here. Some of them have had incredible challenges in their lives, and others received that big "wake-up call" that beckoned them to a greater purpose in life—a calling, not only to take responsibility for their own lives but also to hear the calling of billions of people who are now suffering on this planet, just as they once did. Better yet? *They are taking action by doing something,* day in and day out, and in the process, they are inspiring their sisters and brothers worldwide to the best of their ability.

Each Warrior wants to leave the mark of his will, his signature, on important acts he touches. This is not the voice of ego but of the human spirit, rising up and declaring that it has something to contribute to the solution of the hardest problems, no matter how vexing!
—Pat Riley

Each story is unique. And, each page administrator has a different take on how she or he became happier, peaceful, and more fulfilled as a human being. They share beautiful and loving inspirational truths, and they expose dangerous patterns and hidden agendas that are being used by some of our so-called "leaders" to cause pain and suffering to our fellow humans, to innocent animals, and to this beautiful planet that we call home. These travesties are happening on so many different and toxic levels. As they bravely enlighten their subscribers about these events, they often go to other page administrators for support and guidance. During this process, they are learning, healing, and evolving themselves as well.

I will also share with you that none of them claims to be perfect. They are real, authentic people who are simply committed to improving themselves and their planet as best they can. Just like you and me, they are works in progress. They do their best to "walk their talk" every day. I know this firsthand, because I have seen them live by example, not only via their posts, but also in the backroom of our private Facebook group where all of the authors are invited to network with one another. Thus far, we have seventy-three authors who share and encourage one another, day in and day out. I've witnessed them bring attention to one another's pages with no thought about competition. They believe there is enough for all of us. I've observed them coming to their fellow authors' side when an illness strikes a family, or when a cause encourages their personal help. They are about as authentic as they come.

From my perspective, having the courage to share some of your innermost demons and challenges isn't exactly fun, nor is it effortless. It takes stamina and fortitude to summarize your life purpose—your personal story—in one single chapter. It's far easier to stay hidden behind the scenes and just send out encouraging or controversial posts on the social media stage. Just as I've seen with the amazing authors from *The Faces Behind the Pages That Inspire*—the first book in this three-volume edition—the men and women whom I've asked to write a chapter in this particular book are ready and willing to take their work to the next level. They are willing to do whatever it takes to share their messages with the public, to the point of being willing to expose their innermost selves. They have all done so in this book, with the pure intention of being selfless. For that, I give them an honorable bow as their co-author, and thank them for being willing to *"be the change that they want to see in the world,"* as Gandhi so eloquently put it years ago.

And so, with great hope and excitement for what I feel will indeed touch your heart and inspire you to join us in creating a better world, here's your backstage pass to the faces behind the pages that inspire!

Chapter 1

Meet Lori Rekowski of *A Victim No More*

A Victim No More changed my life, just those four words
have a very powerful message . . . . I know your message
needs to be heard, I am very thankful for this page."
—Connie Pillon

"Why am I such a misfit?
I am not just a nitwit.
You can't fire me I quit,
'since I don't fit in."
—Johnny Marks

MUSIC HAS ALWAYS BEEN a source of hope and healing for me. From the time that I was a child, I've responded to words of songs, such as this particular one from a childhood Christmas classic, "Rudolph the Red-Nosed Reindeer." This song, in particular, resonated with me well into adulthood, as I watched the movie over and over again with my own children. Why? Because, like most of the changemakers on this planet right now—those that have never felt quite right about the social reality that exists today—we have always seemed indeed to feel like a misfit in this world, for as long as we can remember.

I also find it rather humorous that one of the most popular Facebook posts, which gets shared time and time again on various fan pages, says this:

> *The ones that think they are*
> *crazy enough to change the*
> *world are the ones that do.*
> —Steve Jobs

A Victim No More series of books is about how to be inspired to leave the victim mindset—and lifestyle—behind. This series of books, particularly "The Faces Behind the Pages that Inspire," volumes 1 to 3, were created to bring to light amazing and inspirational stories of some very special and powerful changemakers. In the ever-changing world of social media, they are the ones working day in and day out to make a difference. They've created fan pages on Facebook, to inform and inspire their subscribers, and have worked tirelessly behind the scenes to help you and me create a better life.

The co-authors that I chose for this edition are people from almost every walk of life. And believe me, as with the authors from the first in the series, they are passionate and inspired about not only walking their talk, they are doing something about it. You'll read about a once-popular girl (now a 12-year-old powerhouse as she shares her story within these pages) who suffered an 80 percent hearing loss in her elementary years, and how her life was turned upside down and destroyed by this to-date unknown cause. You will be moved by her feelings of hopelessness and suicidal tendencies, because of the cruel bullying by her peers. The amazing inspirational example that she has become will astound you, and the beautiful spirit of those who came to her assistance may bring you to tears. Another inspiring story will move you as the man who nearly lost his life in a tragic auto accident shares how his ordeal turned his life into one of purpose and passion that inspires nearly 100,000 fans daily. You get the point, you are in for a big dose of inspiration that we hope will change your life, too, for the better.

These authors have important messages to share, issues to educate us on, and are *taking action* to inspire others to do the same. They offer a myriad of perspectives on how a person can take a tragedy and turn it into advocacy for others. These brave and dedicated men and women have awakened out of the victim mindset to realize that they are part of a greater whole. These contributing authors are all everyday normal (if there is such a thing) people, just like the rest of us. Yet they have taken their personal tragedies and turned them into triumphs. Better yet, they have owned their responsibility for their own lives and realize now that they are also responsible to their fellow human beings. They believe indeed that no man is an island.

My co-authors in these books have joined me to offer you some assistance in leaving the victim mindset behind you. And even more important, to inspire you not just to think about making this change individually, but as a society, because they have "been there, and done that." They know that part of the journey into healing and finding a purpose in all of this craziness is in giving to others what they've found for themselves.

These stories reflect my personal passion, and that is to serve the purpose of inspiring to leave victimization behind in your own life, and therefore pave the way for a better tomorrow for generations to come. I've definitely brought you some social media experts that are making a *major* and impactful difference in the lives of millions around the world. And when you are finished reading this book, you *will* be inspired by their courage, stamina, and fortitude to overcome their incredible challenges.

As I described in my last book, I have had the gift of psychic abilities since childhood. Years ago, I was given a vision to write a book. I knew as a child that I was going to go through a lot of traumas in my life and I once told my pastor at the age of twelve that I knew this fact, and that I was going to help many thousands of people. Whew! I am glad that I wasn't given the details of what those traumas were going to be! I wouldn't have wanted to "see" what was happening thirty-plus years down the road. I may not have agreed to go through it all if that was the case.

This is why many of us that are intuitive (or "psychic," or whatever you prefer to label it), often are much more accurate and see so much more accurately for others, than ourselves. I am okay with that reality.

There is a mass unrest happening on this planet right now. So what exactly can *you* do about it? What can you do for others when you are often struggling to keep your own life in control. to feel safe and hopeful again?

To begin with, it's about learning to overcome the feeling that your life is "out of control." And most people that I have met do not like the feeling of being out of control. Fear is often the underlying culprit of that feeling. Fear feeds anger, especially if you don't have the tools to deal with it effectively. Most of our educational systems worldwide today don't include lessons on how to handle these emotions, as part of our curriculum. Therefore, we will do our best to be offering you plenty of tools both here in this book and on our Facebook network. Many of my co-authors have classes, YouTube videos, websites, or books they've written in their own area of expertise, interactive groups to join, films, conferences coming to your towns, and so very much more. After you are introduced to this team and their extended work, you will have access to many tools to assist you in shedding the blanket of fear, anger, and pain on our planet. They each have links at the end of their chapters and also on our website, *www.pagesthatinspire.com*.

Getting Back to the Reality of Fear Feeding Anger

Let me return to this topic of fear for a moment, as I feel that it is a very important one to discuss before we all move forward together to be inspired by my fellow authors in this book. So many of us have bouts of feeling powerless and insignificant when we look at this big mess humanity has gotten itself into, so much so that we have just thrown up our hands, or worse yet, gotten stuck in anger about the whole darn mess. Let me run with this idea of fear for a moment here, and paint you a picture of where I am going with this reality that we are all facing together, on this planet today. Fear is a big issue, and there is no denying it, try as you may.

Let's say that you caught the nightly news one day. For months now, you've viewed a report on riots in the streets of a foreign country. You also read about the thousands of people who have lost their jobs and homes in the news feed on your computer's landing page. Okay, you can deal with that. It's not affecting you or your family directly—yet.

And then the next day, you are driving down the neighborhood street and spot an unexpected foreclosure notice on your neighbor's home. You get to work and you hear rumors that the company is considering layoffs. Next thing you know, the news reporter is talking about a group of picketers that are taking over a street in your city! I think that you know where I am going with this . . . it starts to hit home. Fear starts to move in.

And, as much as we may not want to accept that fear arises in *everyone's* life, in today's world, we just can't deny the fact that there is a lot of chaos happening on this planet, and that we will instinctively feel the emotion of fear. Life isn't always fair and the paradigm on this planet definitely isn't one of fairness right now. Period.

If you are human you have a built-in natural fight-or-flight instinct embedded within you. And, as a residual of hearing the repetitive "bad news" come up in our perceptual fields, the resulting primary emotion of fear is arising in many of us. The emotion of anger often surfaces next. And consequently, more and more of us are beginning to feel angry and victimized, and that our lives are out of control. Anger is brewing on this planet and there is no avoiding it.

Harnessing the Power of Anger

One of the primitive functions of an animal's response to fear is to frighten away the attacker. But in modern human life, we often frighten away those who we need and care about most. Besides this, prolonged anger has clear health consequences.

—Dr. Herbert Benson

I find it quite interesting that today, as I was scheduled to write this introduction, I encountered a situation in my own personal life, which gave way to my "experiencing" anger myself. I won't get into the details as to exactly what caused that anger, as that isn't what matters at the moment. What matters is that, since I've learned to leave the old victim pity party that I used to live in my life daily behind, I realize that my learned skill and improved ability to observe the anger, rather than allowing it to ruin my day, is actually a wonderful gift! You see I've learned to embrace the fact that anger isn't a bad emotion. It just "is what it is." No judgment!

I've had more than enough of black-and-white thinking to last a lifetime. What a change that has made for me and those around me, to come to that conclusion! To discover that there actually is a "grey zone" has released the suffocating hold that my old perfectionist, right-or-wrong, victim attitude created for years, and it is very freeing! My self-worth has grown significantly because of this revelation. I've been able to learn to relax and accept life's circumstances so much more effortlessly. The more I have learned to practice these tools, the more I valued myself, the more my self-worth has begun to grow. I am so grateful that I could discover and learn to use tools that would bring me peace of mind. And I am even more grateful that I get to share my lessons and new empowerment practices through my posts on Facebook. You will also be able to observe my co-authors using the same common tools throughout their stories in this book.

In the past, I found that in order to release my need always to feel like I needed to get validation outside myself, I had to learn how to let my emotions become my friends, not my enemy. I had to stop judging myself for having these emotions in the first place. As a child growing up in my world, we didn't air our personal problems or struggles. There was too much shame in the thought of that. Fortunately, our world has evolved somewhat, and society is shifting away from that old way of thinking.

I chose to stop feeling like a ship being tossed around at sea and instead to dig in and get to work. Once I discovered that there is no bad emotion in the first place, I needed to learn how to harness the power of my emotions, and better yet, to learn what these emotions meant, and why they were showing up! Empowerment was within my reach. In fact, I began to feel more and more powerful as I practiced the tools that I taught in my own work, and drew in other like-minded people to practice them with.

I no longer felt that my life was out of control (because I had no clue what to do with my emotions), and as a result, I found that I didn't need to be validated by others as much as I once had. Hence, the pressure to prove myself began to leave me. I also noticed that the need to make myself right, by proving someone else wrong, also waned.

I am fortunate enough now, to know that every emotion serves a purpose in my life. And sometimes it just feels so good to give myself permission just to feel sad or angry, or anything in between! When I was living in the victim mindset, I had no clue how to do that. I only wanted to escape feeling anything! Emotions are our regulators of whether we are acting (or interacting) in a way that is pulling us out of our center. Personally, my center happens to be peaceful a majority of the time now. And, peaceful is a state that I strive to stay in, each and every day.

For me, today, my ability to be mindful of the emotion of anger is, as I said, a "gift" that I am allowing myself to feel. Rather than resist or stuff anger down deep inside myself (where it inevitably comes out at the most inopportune times), I work daily to accept that it is just an emotion. That it is a warning signal that I've been pulled out of a peaceful center or mindset. When I feel anger now, I can disengage and use the warning signal to set *boundaries* with others or in unhealthy situations. And I've thereby changed my experience with the emotion of anger into a powerful tool, by choice.

This reality for me is the perfect example of one simple tool that frees us from the victim mindset. Using your emotions to work *for you*, rather than letting them *control* you. This is a skill that I have begun to master. How? I've practiced it over and over again, and it is now becoming far more natural for me to apply it in my daily life. Of course, I still have a way to go; however, I am deeply committed to mastering this skill. I find that I am also much more willing to express the concerns and confusion that I experience within my relationships, because I feel safer to do so. I trust myself more to express myself better and in a much more noncombative, I-*need*-to-be-right, manner. Communication is, and always will be, the key ingredient to any happy relationship. Living free of the victim mindset offers far more opportunities to engage in drama-free relationships; this I can promise.

The Collective Anger

You and I both know that there are plenty of reasons that people around the world are angry right now. Anyone who is exposed to media of any kind is well aware that there are myriad examples of victimization occurring each and every moment on this planet. Watch the nightly news in any country; read the news headlines on your email provider's landing page, watch the posts heading down your timeline on Facebook, and you will see plenty of examples of anger-provoking stories to view.

> *"Anger comes from judgment and is a weapon*
> *I use against myself, to keep miracles away."*
> —Lesson 347, A Course in Miracles

Yet, to reiterate once more, the primary purpose of this book series is to teach you that you can choose to act and react in any way you need to in the moment, without projecting it onto others. Once we actually can accept the fact that it's okay to feel miserable sometimes, we tend to quit trying to give our power away to others to fix us. The authors in this series have learned firsthand, that *it's all about our attitude.* And so, we will all practice becoming observers here together, as we read the stories of my co-authors and what they are doing about their own anger, hurt, and frustrations.

We will observe here together the many creative and productive ways that they live, by their example, which will show us exactly how they are proactive in dealing with the anger that is permeating our society today. No two stories are the same within these pages. You will also observe through their personal heartfelt stories, how they have taken responsibility for their lives and the betterment of the greater whole.

There are many personalities and various interests within our new global society. There are also many different talents and passions that exist in this group, and these authors recognize that there is no one single path that is right for us all.

I am sure that you will find one that resonates with you personally more than the others. That is a good thing. Diversity abounds within this book, just as it does in the fabric of humanity. There is a common thread that runs through these stories though. and that is love. Every single one of these authors knows that love, not hate; acceptance, not judgment; and forgiveness, not bitterness bring us hope for peace and a better tomorrow, if we can begin to wake up to who we really are. Interconnected beings that long for us all to "just get along and to care for and about our fellow humans." They wish for a new peaceful resolve that will stop the greedy and power-hungry individuals from destroying our planet, and they have hope in mankind that we can yet rise above and turn ourselves around before the planet is destroyed by our disrespect for her resources.

It's been ten years since I received a vision to write my first book, *A Victim No More.* It's been a long journey and one that I must admit hasn't always been an easy one. Digging myself out of the victim mindset was no easy task, especially since I was so deeply immersed in it.

However, I will be the first to admit that living in the victim mindset is exhausting in and of itself. I am grateful that I chose to invest the same amount of energy into turning my life around. The rewards have been tremendous on so very many levels. And frankly I must say that the most rewarding part of the journey has been the opportunity to serve others in the process. I have such a deep sense of joy and peacefulness, when I can hop on my pages and inspire others to rise out of the victim consciousness. The touching responses that I have received from my subscribers have inspired me to keep moving forward.

On days that I struggle with some of life's tough times, I get right in there and share what I'm feeling. I strive to be authentic and to take these challenges and apply the powerful tools that I've learned over the years to overcome them. The responses that I receive from my subscribers are often one of identification and willingness to share their stories or comments in order to help their fellow subscribers and they in turn gain a sense of encouragement when they can do so.

The same goes for my co-authors. Thus far, I've been told that they have taken some of my guidance, inspirations, and insights, as well as inspiration from their co-authors, and applied them to their own lives at times as well. Miracles are occurring within this group behind the scenes of this project already. I've seen many of them blossom into being even more confident and resilient teachers by unifying their efforts and goals by being the great changemakers that they have agreed to be in this lifetime. Each of these authors is incredibly special to me. It is a great honor to have them join me on this mission to free millions of souls from self-sabotage and often a lack of self-worth and to motivate them to become the changemakers who are needed desperately on this planet right now. They are my heroes and I strive to learn and grow from their ability to walk their talk. In fact, I've manifested the most remarkable co-authors that I could ever have dreamed of. May you all be as blessed as I have been, to have read their stories, and to see just how far and high a person can rise after traumas and tragedies.

I wish you all an inspired life, filled with peace of mind and a strong desire to take your own healing and pass it on to those in need.

 Lori Rekowski is a published author, a professional speaker, an advocate for many nonprofit organizations and causes, and is a loving mother and grandmother. She has been a successful business entrepreneur and consultant for more than twenty-five years. She takes great pride in celebrating her healing process with others. In fact, she considers it her life purpose and passion.

A creative and analytical approach to her healing path during the past twenty years included research and participation in the holistic healing field. After years of seeking help from the traditional psychological health field, Lori was unsuccessful at maintaining long-term emotional stability. She knew (had faith) that there had to be a more effective path to emotional and spiritual stability. Lori found that the most effective assistance, allowing her own healing to accelerate, was the research and application of ancient healing modalities that are resurfacing in our society today, integrated with traditional medicine.

Lori studied hundreds of books, experienced private healing sessions, and attended various seminars and classes throughout the United States, internationally, and on the Internet. She focused attention on her own unique inner connection to God and used the spiritual self-help field to heal successfully. This approach and the use of these tools accelerated her healing process at an amazing pace. She looks forward to sharing these tools with other survivors, assisting them in stepping into a healthy and happy lifestyle.

http://www.facebook.com/avictimnomore
http://www.avictimnomore.com
http://www.pagesthatinspire.com
http://www.facebook.com/thefacesbehindthepagesthatinspire
http://www.facebook.com/acourseincourage
https://www.facebook.com/TheLightworkerExpress
https://www.facebook.com/ACourseInCourageVictoryTour

Chapter 2

Meet Daniel Gottwald of *Catalyzing Change*

GROWING UP, I NEVER really learned all that much directly from teachers. I respected their insight, but it was too hard for me to pay attention in class. I was just not interested in the subjects being discussed and I preferred learning alone. I learned to have fun in school and after the school day was over, I would learn at home when I was studying alone.

It was always so strange to me that, in school, we learned what people told us, instead of what we were curious about or what we wanted to learn about. It never made any sense to me. When I was little, I would ask myself the big questions like How do we get to the stars? Where did we come from? Where do people go when they die? When I brought up these questions, people seemed to be afraid or not interested. They would look at me as if no one knew these answers and that it is impossible to find out. So, over many years I learned to suppress these questions that I had as a young child, and instead, I worried about getting good grades, graduating high school, and becoming a great athlete.

I created Catalyzing Change about three years ago in the fall of 2009, but it all really started in November 2006 when one of the most important events of my life occurred. Late night after attending a Boston Celtics basketball game, I was in the back seat of a friend's SUV. We were on our way home when we crashed into a massive puddle, the car flipped numerous times and I was thrown from the vehicle at 70 mph on the Interstate. I landed on the other side of the highway, in the passing lane. I don't remember the accident itself. I remember seeing the big puddle before the crash and then I woke up. The seconds that passed seemed like hours. I felt as though I was somewhere else for a period of time, but then I woke up, dazed and confused.

I was lying in a puddle, looking straight up at the sky, and I couldn't get up. I was cautious to even attempt to move, I could only lie still. It was the strangest feeling. I do not remember being in pain at the time. The driver and two other occupants inside the vehicle suffered minor injuries. They were trying their best to help me out off the road, but I could not move; my back was not working. The first vehicle coming from the opposite direction happened to be a police car. The driver of the first vehicle behind us was a nurse. They both stopped to aid us and I was taken to the hospital. I barely remember the ride, but when I awoke the next day, I understood that I had suffered two broken vertebrate (T-7, T-8) and a severe concussion. The doctors told me that I would have to wear a body cast/back brace for the next few months. I would have to do a lot of resting and did not know if I would recover at all. I would have to become more patient than ever.

My whole life I had been physically active; I played either hockey or baseball every day. It was who I was and I loved it. So, it makes sense that the main message the doctors kept telling me was that I would go through physical therapy and work hard to regain my strength. Trying to comfort me, they told me that my aim was to "get back on the ice." What the doctors and those around me did not understand was that when I awoke from the car accident, I felt like a new person.

The concussion that I suffered seemed to shift the way that I was thinking. I would not be able to drive a car, play catch, or skate at the rink for a long time, but, strangely, I was not worried. Instead, I was questioning things that I hadn't in years. I was excited to connect with my old thoughts. I was asking myself, Where did we come from? Where are we heading? What are we? Who are we? What is really going on? The questions that were important to me as a child were now all I could think about. I realized that these questions did not disappear. They had only been suppressed.

I decided to take advantage of the Internet while my back was healing. The Internet was my type of learning. Self education with a little bit of guidance of my choice. I could choose what I would like to learn about! I literally wrote down almost every question that I could think of about the world and tried to find out if anyone had the answers. The Internet showed me that there are so many answers. Though not all of them may be the correct answers, it was sure interesting to see what people had to say. I found books all over the Internet, YouTube lectures, and websites of the less known authors who have explored these questions. The people that I resonated with most were people that I had never heard of. It was an amazing feeling. I discovered there were so many more mysteries than I ever imagined. And with all that I had discovered, I knew I hadn't even scratched the surface.

My back healed about 80 percent after a year, and I was able to be physically active to a certain degree. But now, instead of watching Red Sox and Bruins games, I continued to watch lectures about ancient history, sacred geometry, numerology, hidden histories, and mysteries. I had discovered what I wanted to do with my life. It was to get the answers to some of the big questions and mysteries. I wanted to share the things that I had learned that are not being shared in mainstream society.

I learned more, alone, in a couple months with the Internet than I had in my whole life in the school system. The most important thing that I learned was that everything I had ever learned was not the truth, it was only a perception. What I had been previously told about history, countries, governments, politics, and humanity had now been completely shattered. Everything was different from what I had previously read and been told. The important people that I had learned about were different. The authors were different. The history was different. Sometime, even the good guys and the bad guys in history were different. Everything was different. It was amazing to learn without so much pressure of receiving a good grade. I could now think what I wanted to think, rather than form a thought or answer that agreed with a textbook.

After discovering some of the beliefs of ancient cultures and people such as Terence McKenna and Gregg Braden, I was suddenly seeing that all is connected. All is One. Everything that we do affects everything else. I was now thinking about the Earth in the way that I was previously programmed to think about only my country. It hit me that I am not only equal with all Americans, but more importantly with all the people of the Earth. With this new sense of understanding, I said to myself, it is time to connect with people from all over the planet.

I found some forums on the Internet where amazing topics were being discussed, from ancient advanced civilizations, advanced technologies, hidden history, and information that is not generally known to the public. It was great to hear ideas that I hadn't previously. I wanted to share some of the ideas that I had come across over the past few years and it was a bit of a hassle having to sign up on each website to be part of a discussion. I thought that others were probably in the same situation as I was, so I created a Facebook page named Catalyzing Change, where we could all share with one another in real time via comments and discussion.

Catalyzing Change is a place for people across the globe to connect, meet one another, and discuss topics that are harder to come by in mainstream society. We give a voice to the lesser known and incredibly important philosophers, scientists, and historians, some who can no longer speak. We discuss ancient cultures from the Mayans, Egyptians, and Sumerians, to the "legends" of Atlantis and Lemuria. We share daily news and discoveries that hardly ever make it into the mainstream news.

I believe that one of the keys to solving the world's problems is simply awareness. I think it is imperative that powerful information such as Nikola Tesla and his scientific discoveries, and Edgar Cayce and his prophecies, be available and taught in schools to those who are interested. Catalyzing Change has given me the opportunity to share my knowledge and to learn directly from thousands of people who have unique insights from all over the planet. The page now has upwards of 40,000 fans and we are sharing more each day!

 Dan grew up the youngest of five children in a suburb just outside of Boston, Massachusetts. He spent the first twenty years of his life as an athlete, dedicated to hockey and baseball. At the age of 21 he went through a near-death experience during a car accident which shifted his focus and made him realize what his mission in life really is: to aim for the big questions in life; to seek the truth about who we really are as human beings and our true history. After searching for answers, he envisioned a new form of education where millions can be reached and shared with over the Internet. Dan created Catalyzing Change to share the knowledge, authors, and researchers he has come across who are harder to come by in mainstream society and who challenge mainstream versions of history.

www.catalyzingchange.org
https://www.facebook.com/pages/Catalyzing-Change

Chapter 3

Meet Shawne Duperon of *Project: Forgive*

From Victim to Warrior

THE PHONE RANG.

It's the call we all dread.

The nurse told my friend Gary Weinstein, there had been an accident and to come to the hospital right away.

He remembers the doctor saying, "We did everything we could, but he didn't make it."

"You mean no one made it?" Gary asked.

"No. No one made it," said the doctor.

Gone in an instant. Gary's wife, Judy, and their two children,12-year-old Alex and 9-year-old Sam, were killed by a drunk driver. Wow. Losing your entire family.

How devastating.

Even though it's been a few years, I remember that day like it was yesterday. It was hard for my family, too, because Gary's family was connected to mine. Judy was my husband's business coach. My kids babysat Sammy and Alex. I remember the deep anguish of that day and I couldn't fathom the pain Gary must have felt losing his entire family.

The story gets even deeper. A few hours after the crash, I received another phone call about the man who killed Gary's family, Tom Wellinger, who also happens to be another dear family friend.

What are the odds of knowing both families?

In that moment an internal dilemma was created for me. On the one hand you have Tom, a drunk driver who killed a family. On the other hand, you have Tom, a loving husband and father who made a horrible and devastating choice to drink and drive.

How do you hold these conflicting emotions within your heart at the same time? I felt deep anger and rage at a man who killed a precious family, and I also felt deep sorrow and compassion for a man who made the mistake of a lifetime—both at the same time.

While many of us won't have to face such a tragedy as Gary's (thank goodness), we all deal with this dilemma at some level. It's a spiritual dilemma requiring emotional maturity, holding two extremely opposite, conflicting feelings at the same moment.

For you, it might be loving your job while despising your boss. Or deeply loving your partner or spouse while also feeling pain at his or her inability to manage money. Or maybe you just received news that you have cancer. On the one hand you're deeply spiritual and trust divine order, while at the same time you're extremely angry at God for giving you this dreadful disease.

Tough stuff. Yep, we all face tough stuff. The question becomes how do we feel, accept, and forgive these battling and conflicting emotions?

From a broader perspective, when you do your own personal healing, you heal the planet. When you complete issues that are incomplete, that's when you become outrageously free to cause global differences, like creating world peace (that's a biggie). And here's the thing: If you can't forgive your ex-spouse, a horrible boss, or a customer who cheated you, how can we, as a global consciousness, forgive greedy corporations, pedophiles, environmental catastrophes, political disharmony, immigration issues, and war?

We can't. As Albert Einstein said, "We can't solve problems by using the same kind of thinking we used when we created them." The ability to hold two very different perceptions at the same moment is where the consciousness shifts and it's where the breakthroughs lie.

For me, it goes back to a painful time in 1972 in Detroit, when I was just 8 years old. I would come home from elementary school and quickly strategize the fastest and safest way to get to my bedroom. My goal was to avoid my stepfather at all costs, who was masturbating or exposing himself on the couch. Sadly, not a typical day for a second grader.

My personal journey moving from victim to warrior is a profound one and I wouldn't trade my life experience for anything. Not that I wish child molestation on anyone. It's a deep wounding that takes a warrior "being" to move through. And I'm a warrior. If you're reading this book, I bet you are, too.

I'm at this exquisite point in my life where I can honestly say incest is the best thing that ever happened to me. I know it sounds odd, and it resonates to my core. Incest molded me; created me; transformed me into a compassionate, loving, spiritually deep woman. Because I speak on the topic of forgiveness, lots of people ask me if I forgave this father figure for wounding me so deeply. I always answer: "Forgiveness is different for everyone. For me, it's about acceptance of what's so. I've accepted and continually claim what happened. It's really that simple for me now."

I can also hold two perceptions *at the same time* about my stepfather. On the one hand I see a man who brutally took my childhood and wounded my sexual identity, impacting my personal power. And on the other hand? I see a small child who came from horrible abuse himself, who in his adulthood didn't heal, causing others pain, and at the same time was doing the best that he could with the skills that he had.

Bottom line? This is my journey and my life. We all have "stuff" that happened to us. When you do your internal spiritual work, such as taking personal development courses or reading transformational books, miracles manifest. Your most horrible life incidents, if you're open to it, can become part of your life's passion and purpose. That's exactly what happened for me.

My purpose is to speak as a communication leader across the globe. With a strong background in film, marketing, and media (I also worked in news for many years), I use universal themes of love, fear, and forgiveness in business communication. I love what I do.

Through my life experiences (which I also call divine intervention), my passion and purpose became quite clear. It also became intertwined with Gary's. Gary's experience became the catalyst for a global movement and a movie on forgiveness, called Project: Forgive.

I produced Project: Forgive's little five-minute video (*www. ProjectForgive.com*), It has been seen by tens of thousands of people, and even went viral without YouTube. We trended on Twitter, were featured in major media including *Inc. Magazine,* flew to New York to be featured on a segment with Soledad O'Brien on CNN, garnered massive press from ABC, NBC, FOX, CBS, numerous radio stations, and newspapers across the United States, and forty newspapers across Canada. One story in the *Detroit Free Press* elicited 11,000 emails alone. At this point, we are receiving a Facebook "Like" every hour. How cool is that?

Who would have predicted Gary's devastating loss would catapult a global movement on forgiveness? Gary exemplifies the skilled ability of emotional maturity. That ability is to feel two (or more!) conflicting emotions at the same time. When he met Tom in prison, Gary's first question to Tom was "Can you forgive yourself? (Go see the entire conversation at the ProjectForgive.com website.)

Isn't that a question you are always asking yourself? Forgiveness equals freedom and takes you from victim to warrior. So how do you get back in your life's groove after something significantly painful happens to you that deeply hurts?

Here are some questions to ask yourself to move through forgiveness, rather than suffer continuously in loss and victimhood:

Ask: *Did I do my absolute best with the skills that I currently have?*

Moving toward forgiveness is a skill. Sometimes we're simply doing our best given the circumstances. You truly can only do your best at any given moment. Acceptance of what "is" will help you move on.

Ask: *Did I learn something significant and grieve my losses?*

The biggest obstacle to freedom within a forgiveness paradigm, is allowing your emotions. When emotions pass through you rather than glob on to you, you gain extraordinary freedom. When you don't grieve your losses, suffering keeps you tied down, inevitably causing you to repeat similar past mistakes.

Ask: *Can I accept my humanity?*

Perfection is overrated. When you strive for perfection, it's inevitable that you'll fail to some degree. You're human. You make mistakes. Others make mistakes. It's simply how life works.

The game is to see it, accept it, grieve it, and move on.

Does it mean you don't have regrets, bouts of anger, feelings of loss that come and go? Of course not. Everyone's forgiveness journey is different.

As I close, I'd like to share about Judy Weinstein, Gary's wife. She was a dynamo leader and a powerhouse coach, too. She actually coached business leaders to move from victim to warrior. If she were here today, this is what she'd say: "So I'm dead. Now what?"

Project: Forgive is my "now what."

What's yours?

 Six-time EMMY® Award winner Shawne Duperon has been in the TV business for nearly twenty years. She has taught thousands how to communicate as leaders using universal themes of love, fear, and forgiveness in the workplace. Shawne works with corporations, entrepreneurs, universities, and government agencies across the globe. Her story of overcoming child sexual abuse has inspired thousands.

She has interviewed many U.S. presidents and has filmed hundreds of celebrities. You've watched her on national networks such as CNN, and CBS *The Early Show,* and have seen her featured in *Inc. Magazine, USA Today, The Washington Post,* and *The Chicago Tribune,* to name a few.

One of her personal passions is the work she does with multicultural groups to help delete media stereotypes through communication leadership. She spearheaded the movement on global forgiveness called Project: Forgive, a little five-minute video that went viral without YouTube!

Shawne is currently a PhD candidate, creating leading-edge research on the relationship between mass media and gossip (yes, gossip!). She says knowing how to create and navigate communication skills as a leader is the secret to unlimited marketing and personal power.

Connect with her on Facebook:
www.Facebook.com/ProjectForgive
www.Facebook.com/ShawneTV
http://www.ShawneTV.com/
http://ProjectForgive.com

Chapter 4

Meet Karleigh Strickfaden, Founder of *Teens Against Cyber Bullying*

Let's start with a quick snapshot from the About section on Kar's page. If you are not inspired yet, then read on? I am so honored to have Kar's story in our book. She is a true living and breathing example of a hero!
—Lori Rekowski

About

Who are we? We're teens, just like you. We're here to change the world, no matter what it takes. But why? Because we've been there. Because we understand. Because you're worth it.

Mission

To help schools and communities become more aware and ensure a safe environment for *all* students, free from harassment, physical altercations and neglect. To protect students from *all* forms of peer abuse including, physical, verbal, and electronic harassment, and from neglect at their schools and throughout their communities, or by those who have been entrusted by their parents who trust these people with keeping their children safe and have their well-being in mind.

My Story:

As many know, I'm the owner and founder of an organization called TACB (*Teens Against Cyberbullying*), am involved with several organizations, including something called *Break the Grey*. TACB is an all-teen-run organization, put together by me when I was just 11, and run by teens from about ages 11 to 18. Despite our name, we don't talk only about cyberbullying, we also talk about anything today's society is facing: eating disorders, addictions, drugs, cutting, abuse, etc. We bring awareness and prevention to several topics by going to schools and speaking, speaking at churches, as well as, mentoring several teens online and offline. Now you may be asking yourself, "Why would an 11-year-old start a big organization like this?

Well, let me tell you my story.

When I was around 6 years old, I completely lost my hearing in my right ear, and I could hear only 10 percent in my left. The audiologists had no scientific explanation as to why or how I went deaf, so they equipped me with hearing aids and left. Let me remind you that I was pretty popular at that age—kids would always want to be around me. However, after I got my hearing aids, nobody liked me anymore. I felt so . . . alone. Every day, I was called fat, ugly, worthless. You name it: I was probably called it! The teachers did nothing about it, telling me they were just words, and it didn't matter. Yeah, they're just words, but they *hurt!* Not too long after that, I started getting harassed online as well. All I could think was, "What's *wrong* with me? Why did *I* have to become deaf?!" I began skipping school, missing 150 days in the fifth grade. I was often suicidal, and started cutting myself. I felt as if life just wasn't worth it anymore, nobody liked me. I was now in the sixth grade, more suicidal than ever. I had a plan to kill myself, and I thought it through every day. The day in sixth grade when I planned to kill myself an organization called Break the Grey came to my school. Bill Ballenger, the owner and founder of Break the Grey, dug himself in a deep hole, lost his baby girl, and ended up in jail. Everything he said just spoke to us students. His story touched us, the fact he actually *cared* touched us. I still remember the words he spoke that saved my life:

"You're probably sitting here thinking, 'what's my life worth? Nobody likes me, nobody cares... I might as well end it all.' But, let me tell you something: it's not going to be easy hanging on, but it's going to be worth it. You may think ending your life will solve everything, but just wait one more day. I'm so sick of this generation going down the drain, and I'm ready to take a stand. But you're all going to have to take the first step."

When he walked into my school, I had already started my organization, and had given it up immediately. I hated the bullying it brought. But what Bill said to me left me in *tears*. I decided to keep on living, and share my testimony, reaching out to other kids, just as the guy who saved my life did. Back then, I never knew I would be involved with his organization, but I *did* know I was going to keep on supporting him.

Now, here I am, mentoring to students in my school, giving counselors advice on how to speak with someone about something, giving teachers advice, and mentoring kids online. It's something I never would have thought would happen. I thank God every day that He gave me the chance to work with such amazing people, to be able to reach out to kids at my age, and to be able to make a difference.

Now, whether you're young or old, in America or another country, I just want you to know this: It *can* and it *will* get better! Don't be afraid of taking a stand; just go ahead and do it!

The movement starts with you.

Karleigh Strickfaden
Owner/Founder
TACB (Teens Against Cyber Bullying)

 Kar is a 12-year-old girl who has only 20 percent of her hearing. She was bullied from the time she was in first grade until she decided to stand up for herself and others by starting her own organization to stop bullying in middle school. She is an amazing young girl who believes in herself and speaks her truth.

https://www.facebook.com/TeensAgainstCyberBullying/info
https://www.facebook.com/LoveisLouderThanBullying

Chapter 5

Meet Richard Crawford, Four-time Emmy Award Winning Filmmaker and Wisdom Teacher

MEETING LORI REKOWSKI through a mutual friend on Facebook was one of those "meant to be's" that the universe aligns for us. It was actually through one of my fellow authors in this book, Cathy Austin. I remembered once again that there are a myriad of synchronicities happening (far beyond what most of our us are consciously aware of or able to comprehend), which are being orchestrated in order for us to live our life's purpose fully. And, as for Facebook? It's actually my wife, Sally, who is the expert in social media, not I. We work as a team, and as my best friend, business partner, and advocate for my work, Sally is the key to my sharing my work as a four-time Emmy Award winning filmmaker in the Facebook venue.

When I discovered Lori's bold mission to work hard at healing the victim consciousness in our society, I simply couldn't resist being a part of that. The first time that we spoke on the phone, we intuitively knew that we were meant to work together. I've actually worked with some of the most well-known authors, teachers, and speakers in the self-improvement genre because of my personal desire to focus my talents, skills, and hard-earned wisdom to be of service to others. I have been behind the camera (and scenes) for most of my career, and I decided that through this project, it was time to step forward and share my personal story of tragedy and the subsequent healing that came out of it. It was painful to actually go back and relive it in order to share it with you all. Yet I am doing so, with great hope and a direct intention of assisting others on their journey.

Now, as we all realize, it often takes a tragedy for humans to understand our life purpose. Life throws something at us that stops us dead in our tracks. We cannot bear the emotional burden alone and have no choice but to seek assistance from outside of ourselves. Often, it is a cry out to God. The "why me's" become the norm during this process. And in the end, it's up to us to find the true lesson that most often comes out of how we *decide* to view the experience of these tragedies. Do we get stuck in the pain or sorrow, or do we move through it to the other side into acceptance? Do we remain the victim of our circumstances or do we garnish the purpose of it and move past just surviving through it to being able to thrive in our lives once again? Most often, albeit painfully so, we realize that the purpose of these tragedies is to wake us up to the fact that we are spiritual beings living in physical bodies. We are here to love life, to feel life, and to fully experience all that it brings us. Once we are ready, we realize fully that our purpose is to serve and enjoy this gift of life that we've chosen to live. With that being said, I am honored to share the most painful experience of my own life in hopes of inspiring you all to understand the immeasurable unconditional love that is always available to us if we choose to accept it.

If the Sky Should Fall

Sally, my love and girlfriend of a year, brought her 5-year-old son and joined me with my two teen daughters on a great adventure. Every summer, for seven wonderful years, we made our way across America by working with fairs and carnivals. We wanted to experience the fullness of life and enjoy the beauty of the American landscape. No more working eight hours in a cubical at a corporation. We were free and on the road to find out!

On the Fourth of July we were at the Jamestown North Dakota Fairgrounds. The carnival "ride jockeys" shut down the thrill rides, darkened the tower lights, and the carnival closed at midnight. The carnies could now celebrate after hours. Cherry bombs burst, firecrackers exploded, and Roman candles belched rainbow fireballs as the liberated carnies waged Independence Day war.

I was putting my 3-year-old daughter, Sidra, to bed in our motor home. "Daddy read me a story 'bout the bumble bee...Buzz Buzz Bee." I tickled her and marveled at how her Shirley Temple curls jiggled with her laughter. "Okay punkin', I'll sing you a song... you go to sleep now. "Okay, Daddy. Sing the barrel of monkeys song."

"What...oh, okay.

We ain't got a barrel of money, maybe we're ragged and funny, but we'll travel along singing our song side by side. Through all kinds of weather, what if the sky should fall, we'll still be together ...'cause it really doesn't matter at all.

"G'night sweetheart; see you in the morning light." She was fast asleep. I then joined Sally and the kids outside to enjoy the beautiful star spangled summer night. "Sidra's asleep, all tucked in." "I think she'd stay up all night if you let her."

Out of the nearby darkness a running silhouette approached, excited, shouting," Hey Richard, you and Sally gotta see this...it's the Northern lights go'in off...freakin' blazin'-amazin'! C'mon, hurry!"

"Sally, get the kids. I'll just lock up real quick." "Let's go." "What about Sidra?" "She's fine. We're just going across the way for a few minutes."

The sky was ablaze, a tumbling, cascading river of color—actinic blues, roiling reds, splashes of purple, green, and violet—flowing, like oils in a psychedelic light show, oozing to the horizon. "Oh my God, Sally, I've never seen anything like this! Wow!" "Ohhh, it's so beautiful, just amazing," Sally said. Renee chimed in "The colors are just pouring from the sky . . . takes my breath away." Tommy just jumped and ran around in circles bathed in rainbow colors.

The small crowd huddled together, oohed and ahed louder than after the fair's fireworks finale. God had once again topped man's best efforts at spectacle.

Then a shrill voice shattered the dream, "Come quick...your motor home's on fire! Hurry! They're trying to get the door open!" "On fire? What . . . oh, God, Sidra!" Instant fear sucked reality into a small dark tunnel and filled the space with darkness and pain. I couldn't breathe as we all ran to the motor home. I was in a nowhere zone and running in slow motion.

The carnival's strongman, Moose, burst through the doorway of the motor home with Sidra in his arms, alive and crying. The smoke pursued Sidra only to vaporize into the night. Fear gripped my chest, locking my lungs so I couldn't breathe. "This can't be happening. My sweet girl! Oh God!"

The carnies joined the firemen to put out all but the last reluctant embers of the fire. Sally instantly took charge of the kids. "Richard, it's going to be all right. You stay with Sidra and I'll meet you at the hospital with the kids. Don't worry, I love you!"

Sidra suffered burns over much of her body. In the Jamestown emergency room we stood and watched in horror as the medical staff used scissors and knives to remove her burned clothing stuck to her skin. "Daddy, don't let them hurt me." "Daddy's here sweetie, it'll be all right." I was about to pass out and had to rush out of the room into the night so I could attempt to breathe.

The pain and grief overtook me, with outstretched arms I screamed into the black North Dakota night. The sky had fallen. I fell to my knees and began to sink below the asphalt of the parking lot, crying—out of control, out of my mind, and melting like the bad witch from Oz.

Sally rushed to my side. I was no longer there. I was hidden below the surface, a prisoner of my shame and guilt, as low as I could go. Only death could find me now. "Richard, Richard. I'm here with you, I love you, please, please, we'll get through this."

Sally's alarmed voice, smothered, as if in hurricane winds, barely audible, was calling me back. "It's not your fault! You've got to go with Sidra now. They're flying her to St. Paul for emergency treatment. She's prepped and ready to go."

With a jolt I was back in my body, I could see Sally crying and pleading with me. "Get up! Now! Please, she needs her dad! You have to fly with her. Help her!" My legs lifted me up. I devoured her hug and cried in her arms. The air entered my lungs like the first breath of a baby. The swirling black phantoms vacated my skull and I was back!

The small town hospital staff loaded Sidra and me into a *Cessna*. The pilot fired up the engine and we leapt into the midnight darkness on a wing and a prayer. I held her hand en route to the emergency burn center in St Paul. Paramedics fed life-saving fluids, and anesthetics into Sidra's body, comforting her the best they could.

She had suffered third- and fourth-degree burns over 75 percent of her small body. Sidra would have to undergo a transfusion of blood and extreme emergency treatment in an attempt to keep her alive.

A carnival truck driver rushed Sally and the kids to St. Paul to join me the next day. The doctors were barely able to keep Sidra alive, and painful uncertainty lay ahead. She desperately needed a blood transfusion, a rare blood type that only her birth mother possessed. Her mother was on vacation camping somewhere in California, and no one knew where! The California Highway Patrol began the monumental task of searching the state parks.

Our family lay sprawled on the motel floor across from the hospital where Sidra was being treated for her burns. After unloading the feelings of guilt and responsibility that we all shared, we closed our eyes, imagined a healing, and concentrated on sending energy to Sidra. We applied a very intense form of affirmative prayer, not asking for help, but rather being in gratitude for the healing that was sure to follow.

When I told the doctor about the healing we were sending, he replied, "It's surprising but she is getting better, so whatever you're doing, keep it up; something's working." Two days later the CHP officers found Sidra's mom in a campground and immediately flew her to the St. Paul hospital. At last our prayer treatment bore fruit, Sidra would be getting her mother's blood, which she desperately needed.

The transfusion was working, restoring energy and strength to Sidra. Hope at last. The Red Cross took care of our needs, providing us with food, shelter, and transportation for the next month so we wouldn't worry. The carnies put a collection jar at the cook house and raised much needed money to help us with medical expenses. The team of doctors was determined to save Sidra. The hospital, knowing our financial situation, never brought up the subject of paying the soon-to-be enormous bill. We were blessed.

Sidra endured the horrors of the painful, abrasive, skin-scrapes necessary to prevent scarring. Without her top layer of skin to protect her, she had to fight infectious bacteria that tried to kill her. The doctors did not give her much of a chance to live through it.

Over the next thirty days it was a horrendous roller coaster ride. One day she was showing signs of recovering and the next fighting for her life against infection. Sidra's mother, grandmother, brother, and sisters were there for her through the ordeal. We knew we had to let go of blame and petty thoughts of right and wrong and give Sidra the complete attention she needed to get a healing. Tension was thick in the air during the tumultuous emotional experience.

Then miraculously Sidra was getting markedly better. The doctors were at last optimistic that Sidra was stable enough to prepare her for departure. We began making arrangements to transport her to a Shriner's Burn Center to begin necessary skin grafts to give her new skin protection.

At last, light at the end of the tunnel. The doctors suggested that we return to the carnival, finish our business and make ready to transport Sidra for treatment. With a sigh of relief we returned to our former life and began the difficult task of cleaning up after the fire, to get back to some form of normal life.

Returning to the scene of the fire was painfully difficult, seeing the scorched interior, the burned blankets and toys, and having to breathe in the awful smells of the melted reality that was once our home. Despite all that, we were grateful for the promise of Sidra's recovery. And then a phone in the carnival office rang and sent a messenger to us bearing bad news.

"The hospital just called and said that you better get back there right away. Your daughter has contracted a massive infection; she's in a coma and is not expected to live more than eight hours!" The bottom fell out. Once again I got that sinking feeling. How can this be happening? Didn't the doctor say she was going to be all right?"

We brought the family together to break the news. We'd all been through a lot dealing with the reality of the situation. My daughter, Beth, who has had her share of difficulties having been born with cerebral palsy, offered "If Sidra lives or dies...doesn't she have anything to say about it? Maybe she would rather move on than go through what she'll have to deal with."

Sally followed with: "Beth has a point, maybe we should consider Sidra's feelings, I know we all want her to live. And maybe, just maybe we're hanging on to her, and we each in our own way have to let her go." Renee chimed in, "I don't want her to die...don't you think that's up to God?"

The whole family gathered around Sidra. The life monitor beeped lightly in the background as we all told Sidra what was on our hearts, gave her our blessings. and let her go. Sally was the last to speak. "Though you're not my daughter, I love you very much. I wish for you what you want for you. I release you and let you go. I love you."

Two heart monitor beeps broke the silence and the final beep extended and filled the room with a message of the inevitable. Sidra had made her transition. The sobs and tears were bittersweet. The three years she had been with us were filled with joy, happiness, and the experience of an extraordinary old soul in a giggly body who came briefly to show us who we truly are, to teach unconditional love, to give us the gift of her unique presence, and her love. All were touched and changed.

The ensuing years brought much growth and deeper understanding to all of us. Some events were extraordinary. After Sidra's passing, Sally and I returned to the burned-out motor home. While I was away Sally experienced a transcended moment. "I was dazed and confused. I felt Sidra was my daughter and I had lost my one chance to have another child like her. My life had drastically changed. Then, in the depth of my sadness, cloudiness appeared before me as Sidra. The feeling that enveloped me was of extreme love as if Jesus were there comforting me." The apparition of Sidra said "Everything is going to be all right. You will have more children and you will recognize one as special. Not to worry."

It can take a long time to heal the wounds of the loss of a child. Fourteen years after Sidra's passing, I found myself in the home of a sweet elderly lady, Adelle Tinning. She was a psychic who gave readings and delivered healings through the medium of her drop-leaf kitchen table.

Once Adelle placed her hand on the table it would vibrate and raise two legs up off the floor nearly two feet while the other legs remained on the floor. The 80-pound table had no means of visible support.

I came to her table seeking advice on a difficult decision as to which of three creative ideas for films should I concentrate my energy on? Adelle was always tuned into information from the other side. She would cock her head slightly and listen. And then came this; "There is someone here who is available for you to talk with if you like. Her name is Sid . . . what? Sidra. Do you know anyone by that name?" I was stunned and exhilarated. I said, "Yes, that is my daughter's name. She passed away when she was three. Feel free to talk with her if you like."

The feeling of guilt and responsibility rose to the surface. "I want you to forgive me for whatever I did that might have led to the situation of your death." The table would tap out an answer. One hit to the floor meant no! Bam. One hit. My mind went immediately to "I am wrong, I knew it." Before the thought had barely formed, Adelle said: "She says that you do not need to be forgiven; you did nothing wrong."

She says, "You don't remember that before you came into this world you made an agreement with me. I chose the circumstance of my death; in fact, I planned it!" My mind was reeling and all I could think was that she sacrificed herself for me. She must have heard me. "No, you don't understand; my death was my gift to you."

That did not register. That is like trying to comprehend that a star you see doesn't exist anymore. I am just seeing the light from millions of years ago!" I could feel myself going deaf and blind. "I don't understand!"

Adelle clarified, "She wants you to know that when you came into this life, you wanted to feel the depth of your emotions. She say, 'the fire that led to my death was the best way that I could give that gift to you. It was not a sacrifice but my gift!'"

Since then my life has focused on understanding this concept. It is a real game changer about the reality of this life and those who have come and gone. And since this was revealed to me, I have had the experience of people who have lost a child or a loved one seek me out without knowing my Sidra story.

By sharing my story I have assisted many to move past their guilt and responsibility in the death of a loved one. I simply say, "In your own way talk to your child or deceased loved one and take a moment and thank them for the gift that they gave you." I would ask, "Since the passing of your loved one, has anything changed in your life, have you quit a job you hated or were done with, have you gotten involved in helping or comforting others with a similar challenge?"

If your life has changed for the better then that is the gift. Most people who have had a tragedy in their lives, at about ten years after begin to realize the blessing that came from the experience. Life is a mystery and by definition we will never know all the answers. And yet we can be open for better understanding and begin to see the gifts in our adversity. Sometimes we just don't have the eyes to see nor the ears to hear. We are not victims!

 *Richard Crawford*: Producer, Director, Filmmaker
Sally Crawford: Producer
Richard's and Sally's multi-faceted careers encompass the Amusement business, filmmaking and interactive multimedia.

Richard began his career producing film reports for NASA and the Air Force for the space program. He then went on to do national TV commercials for Ford and Eastman Kodak, Arco, and others.

In addition to his corporate and commercial work Richard produced and directed, the award winning *Captain Milkshake*, the first dramatic full length motion picture to deal with the controversial issues around the Vietnam War. *Captain* was recently, screened as a special guest presentation at the Viennale, Rotterdam, and Leeds International Film Festivals.

Richard along with his wife Sally designed, built and internationally toured the world's first laser multimedia theater, *Laserdome*. The 450 seat mobile theater played to audiences for 3 years across the country and in Canada and Mexico. Richard explored consciousness development with the early pioneers from Esalen and others including: Ida Rolf, Fritz Pearls, Henry Kellerman, Bill Gault, Alan Watts, Timothy Leary, Bernie Gunther and others.

Produced/directed the Terry Cole-Whittaker National TV program. The program was the first to introduce "new thought" weekly to Americans. The program was distributed into 450 markets and had a viewing audience of over 2 million. Sally Crawford headed up the fulfillment depart and coordinated and supervised all orders, correspondence, handling and shipping of all orders, requests, data entry and mail communications with the audience. Richard won an Emmy Award for outstanding religious program and a 2nd Emmy for the animation sequences used in the program. During this period Richard was associated with many celebrities and notables in the new thought movement including, Gavin Mc Cloud, Dennis Weaver, Tony Robbins, Shirley Mc Lain, Dianne Grey, Jerry Jampolski, and others.

Richard and Sally were founders of the New Age School that operated successfully for 3 years and established a landmark for alternative, loving learning under the curriculum and leadership of Joyce Chapman. Later while working with Neale Donald Walsch. Richard revived the The New Age school concept into its next expression, Heartlight.

Richard continued his career doing broadcast segments for programs such as That's Incredible. His work with interactive multimedia training for such companies as Apple Computer, IBM, Ford and Nissan won Richard several Cindy Gold awards for excellence in the media. His 8 years of pioneering in interactive multimedia for training and education has earned his work a place at the *Smithsonian Institute* as an example of this medium. In 1987 Richard was the first American director to produce a joint Soviet-American documentary, *Americans and Glasnost*.

Richard served as the head of Staff for Recreation Foundation for the internationally famous author, of *Conversations With God*, Neale Donald Walsh. There he co-facilitated retreats with Neale and produced and directed television programs, audio books, multimedia and was in development of the feature film *Conversations With God*.

Present Richard and Sally have expanded their ONE Productions corporate communications division to assist start up and second round funding companies in raising capital for growth and development. In the last five years ONE Productions video presentations have assisted several companies to raise more than $100 million dollars for their projects using their videos as the primary capital presentation.

The company's Entertainment division, *Rainbow Star Entertainment* is developing conscious thought programming for Lisa Nichols, one of the stars of The Secret and frequent guest on such shows as *Larry King*, and *Oprah Winfrey*. We are producing an ongoing documentary of her work with teens through her Motivating The Teen Spirit program. Recently the company produced the most recent DVD with Dr. Michael Beckwith, *Pillars of Transformation*.

The company's motion picture studio, Dreamtime Global Cinema is developing a slate of five feature films. It's next picture, *Glorious Wings*, is in production development and is due to start production in the summer of 2010.

Crawford's national clients include; IBM, Ford, Nissan, Apple, Kodak, NCR, Ernst & Young, among others. Richard's awards include four area Emmy Awards, 4 Gold Cindy Awards for multimedia, 4 Tellies, San Diego Film Festival Prize and the New York Art Director's Award. Recently the Piano Wizard Infomercial won the highest award, the Silver Telly, in the infomercial category. Richard and Sally serve as directors of their Humanitarian Collective, an international foundation with programs for disaster relief and social change. Richard is currently the Director for Development for the OITC Global Education Network.

Chapter 6

Meet Valerie R. Sheppard of
The Heart of Living Vibrantly

Shed Your Masks and Be Who You Really Are

I NEVER SAW THE masks I was wearing while I was wearing them. Even when looking directly at myself in the mirror, they were not there. It wasn't until I was willing to take them off that I could see how they had been hiding and protecting me. What I believed then was that who I was being was exactly who I was. What I know now is that it was far from the truth.

The experience that shook me enough to be the "wake-up call" involved a 2005 visit to the Hoag Hospital emergency room, fearing I was having a heart attack. I was accomplished and successful, but as I lay there, hooked up to machines monitoring my vital signs, I couldn't help but wonder, at what cost? My life as a corporate vice president felt too hard, and I really wanted out. At the same time I was judging myself for not feeling grateful for the success I had attained, and afraid of losing it all. Like a lost little girl, I was hiding from making the choices I needed to make and hoping it would just fix itself.

I was *forced* to reflect. "Is this it?" I asked. "Is this what my entire life is going to be about—hard work and struggle to attain outer position, prestige, and financial success, while feeling sad, scared, and lonely on the inside?" I heard myself say, "Where the hell am I?!" which was quickly followed by "No, *who* am I?" And like a key going home in a lock, the pieces of my personal renaissance of being started to fall into place, and the masks could stay invisible no more.

What I know now is that I was attached to personality, identity, beliefs, and story that were the foundation for the false masks that I wore—and they were powerful in my life. I created them through the twists, turns, ups, and downs of my life, and they became the outward expression of what I *thought* was my inner truth as if they were the totality of me. They gave me a place in the world.

I felt secure relating through a title or a salary. I measured myself against others through my collection of stuff or my address. I felt belonging through my personality traits or my credentials. I felt worthiness and confidence from my accomplishments and success. And I tried to hide the color of my skin under all of it. This helped me see where I fit, and where I didn't. These coping behaviors—the masks—became like a favorite old sweatshirt that makes us feel comfortable and safe.

Interestingly, and just like a sweatshirt, these created pieces of ourselves can go only so far in hiding what's underneath. Under the surface, I wasn't really feeling the confidence, strength, security, and worthiness that my outward thoughts, feelings, and actions would suggest. What was hidden from the world, and ultimately what I was hiding from, was a deep-seated idea of myself as being less than—unlovable and unworthy. I experienced early in my life the feelings of never being smart enough, talented enough, Black enough or White enough to be accepted, fulfilled, and happy. I knew something wasn't right, but I thought it was with the world around me. I had no idea the trouble was within.

I grew up in two different cultures. First, I was a Black child born in the beginning of the 1960s. My parents were god-fearing, hard-working, good-hearted people from inner city Baltimore. Born in the 1930s, they'd lived through the dynamic and sometimes most horrific and frightening aspects of the Civil Rights Movement. Marches, lynchings, bombings, riots, and assassination were prominent throughout their youth and young-adult lives. It affected them and washed all over me. I often heard the adults saying things like, "Black people have to work twice as hard to get half as much." At a very young age, I picked up how difficult and potentially deadly it was to be a Black person. My early years were full of discipline, manners, and responsibility as my parents taught me how to measure up in ways I could control.

The second culture in our household was that of a disciplined, high-expectations, career Marine father. Dad was a Mustang—one who enlisted at age 18, and instead of going to officer candidate school, he worked his way up through the enlisted ranks and was eventually promoted to officer. In other words, he got to captain the *hard* way. Military life was filled with separation because of my father's active duty service in Vietnam, we moved a lot, and often lived on military bases. I didn't dare talk back, I answered everything with "sir/ma'am," and I learned a "proper" handshake when I was under 5 years old.

It's no secret that children pick up "lessons" even when no one is teaching. I felt separate as a young girl, and believed I would forever be measured *first* by the color of my skin. Not surprisingly, some of the personality masks I wore became visible at an early age. I declared my independence with "Let Valerie do it!" as a toddler, the first expression of the "independent, strong woman" I was to be labeled later in life. The many moves we made as a Marine Corps family exacerbated the separateness I already felt, and I experienced an almost constant undercurrent of fear. Fear of not being liked, of being alone, and leaving right when I'd finally made a good friend. And perhaps most deeply, I felt uncomfortable in my chocolate brown skin.

Along with the lessons, I made subconscious choices about how to control my experiences. If I was going to stand out, it would be for things that would help me feel secure and loved. I learned to work hard, take charge, and *excel* so there'd be plenty of things to measure beyond the color of my skin. To overcome my fear of power being used against me, I became competitive, aggressive, and driven as I focused on powerfully telling the world who I was and what I was capable of.

I made honor rolls and won track and field records and soccer trophies. I was named captain of this, director of that, and was labeled smart cookie, talented athlete, and leader. I had friends, and we shared laughter and adventures, and yet, I never really felt a sense of belonging. The accomplishments and success were fulfilling for short periods of time, but they weren't enough to fill up what I felt was missing inside me. Regardless of the accolades and recognition I received, I never believed *my* A's, bright ideas, disciplined behavior, and top-notch abilities were treated with the same respect and adoration given others around me.

Throughout it all, I sort of stuffed the sadness, fear, and anger I was feeling and believed I was happy. I figured if I just resisted the thoughts and memories that didn't feel good, I would one day be delivered to my promised land. My grandmother had given me a subscription to *The Daily Word* when I was 13, and I read it every day to stay positive and hopeful, and I rose above—or so I thought.

The me-masks I created followed me into college, graduate school, and my career, where it was more of the same. I was driven to excel and pushing to be recognized and feel lovable. I continued to stuff my feelings, which filled my heart with painful conflict and made my intuitive voice harder to hear and less clear. Instead, I developed a pattern of overvaluing my head's rational guidance. I had invested a lot in developing my logical, analytical, left brain. As a result, my choices generally reflected what I thought I needed to do to be accepted by others, rather than what my true inner self knew or wanted. I was looking outside of me for everything I thought I needed to feel whole—belonging, love, acceptance, happiness, intimacy, security—and I was holding everyone in my life responsible for giving it to me.

In 2004, after an award-winning, fast-track corporate ascent, I landed at what I thought was *the* pinnacle of my career: I was offered a vice president of marketing role in a sixteen-billion dollar company, running a large portfolio of regional and national brands. I started this new adventure in bright-eyed excitement. But what I thought would be a fairytale quickly became my worst nightmare.

The knowledge and capability I'd brought with me wasn't working as well as it had before. I dug in and worked harder, fighting the anger and resentment that was welling up inside me, and crying by the time I made it to my car almost every night. I was not even close to happy, but I plodded on, determined to make it work, adamant that I would find a way to demonstrate that I was up to the task.

Somewhere around the 459th day of agony, which is where this story started, I made a conscious decision to say, *enough!* I was tired of the struggle, pushing and proving. I was tired of the self-abandoning choices. I was weary of the victimization I was inflicting on myself, and I was desperate to understand where it all came from and why I was doing it.

I gave myself a radical sabbatical, trading in my corporate persona for a journey into the spiritual aspects of me. I spent the first three years discovering all the masks, then unraveling the false beliefs that had put them into place and kept me running ragged. I know now the power of the sacred heart and choose to express from that part of me more consciously, using my head as a secondary source of wisdom and guidance. I root my thoughts, feelings, and actions in a belief system based in divine wisdom instead of worldly experience, universal law instead of man's law.

I've connected deeply to the true me, the magnificent essence that is my natural beingness of peace, love, joy, and freedom. This is true for you, too. This is not some faraway experience that we have to strive for or prove to others we deserve. We already are those things. There's never anything missing from inside any of us. What's missing is the connection to or alignment with our essence.

We get there by focusing on the relationship we keep with *ourselves.* It influences and impacts everything we experience. How well we know, honor, nurture, forgive, and love ourselves is being reflected back to us in all our outer experiences and relationships. Yet we are taught that it's selfish and potentially even narcissistic to spend time in relationship with ourselves. Instead, we learn to focus outside, expecting love and happiness from others, working to please others, and making our lives about being responsible for others.

We must push past this, and *any* learned belief systems that force us to take a backseat in our own lives. Only a healthy and responsible focus on ourselves enables us to express the whole and complete beings that we are, enabling us to give ourselves in service and in love to others.

Ultimately, we can only hide from truth for so long. Each time I thought I'd overcome whatever or whoever wasn't working in my life, the fear, sadness, and unworthiness always came right back. It was like the hidden part of an iceberg, a massive obstacle right under the surface. Confucius said, "Wherever you go, there you are." When something is a part of the "you-ness" of you, like a belief system, it is with you always. You can move to another state, change schools, leave relationships, and accept other jobs, but it won't make a difference. The trials and tribulations in your life are your soul's call into awareness that it's an iceberg. Until you're willing to chip away at it, heal the wounds, and shed the masks it created, your life will be less vibrant, successful, and fulfilling than it deserves to be.

Florence Henderson once said, "It takes courage to be happy." She was referring to confronting icebergs. By shifting your expression of you, you create a different experience of your life. Root that expression in the truth of who you are, and be joyful, peaceful, and free!

 Sherpa of Happiness Valerie René Sheppard is a recovering corporate executive on radical sabbatical, who is now devoted to guiding people to create success and fulfillment through experiencing authentic happiness. She has developed a signature 4-step process called "Happy to Be ME!" that helps her clients get and stay happy no matter what is going on around them. Valerie has a diverse coaching background spaning more than 25 years, including working with adolescent girls, homeless women, college students, and adult professionals. She is a certified Sacred Contracts coach through the Caroline Myss Education Institute, and has been trained in compassionate communication, spiritual direction and HeartMath. Valerie speaks to numerous audiences, including

corporations, spiritual groups, and major universities, and she has been praised for her speaking and coaching abilities by clients and peers.

Valerie is a 2012 nominee for the *Orange County Business Journal's* Women in Business Award, and the National Association of Female Executives Rising Star Award. She is a national best-selling author with Greg S. Reid of *Everything is Subject to Change*, and is a co-author with Marsh Engle of *Amazing Woman, What's Your Story?* In addition to two eBooks, Valerie has also been published in award-winning *11:11*™ *Magazine, Ezine, Divine Caroline*™, *Light Vision Post*™, and *The Natural You*™. She is based in San Clemente, California where she meditates on the beach and is excited about the release of her latest book, *The Happy to Be ME! Handbook*© due out in 2013. For more information, you can visit her website at *http://heartoflivingvibrantly.com/*. To join Valerie on a Happiness retreat, visit *http://HappinessSabbatical.com*.

Valerie R. Sheppard
Transformational Speaker, Author, Consultant
San Clemente, CA

http://www.facebook.com/heartoflivingvibrantly
http://www.facebook.com/vrsheppard
http://HeartofLivingVibrantly.com
http://twitter.com/ValerieSheppard

COMING SOON:
http://heartoflivingvibrantly.com/happy-to-be-me-handbook

"As long as you live, keep learning how to live."
—Seneca, c. 4 BC-65 AD, Roman Dramatist, Poet and Statesman

Chapter 7

Meet Michele Peterson of Sports Mom Café

"Sports remain a great metaphor for life's more difficult lessons. It was through athletics that many of us first came to understand that fear can be tamed; that on a team the whole is more than the sum of its parts; and that the ability to be heroic lies, to a surprising degree, within."
—Susan Casey, former managing editor of *Sports Illustrated Women*

As a sports mom, I firmly believe in the power of sports to be a positive force in the growth and personal development of children. Unfortunately, the adults involved in youth sports often get in the way.

I created my Facebook page, *Sports Mom Café*, and its corresponding website to be a resource of support, inspiration, and empowerment for sports moms (and dads, too). I hope to encourage positive, conscious sports parenting by reaching out to like-minded parents and by being an example to others of what might be, should be, *must* be.

My passion for this subject stems from my own experience throughout the past six years as a sports mom. In that time, I've witnessed moments of true greatness in the world of youth sports. I've also come face to face with some of the heartbreaking realities of this same world.

I've seen coaches and parents—those who are supposed to be positive role models of sportsmanship—get thrown out of games for unsportsmanlike conduct and other poor judgment. I've seen coaches get so carried away by their own competitiveness that they forget their roles as teacher and mentor; these coaches yell, belittle, and attempt to shame young players into better performance. (By the way, I've never seen this strategy actually work!)

These coaches see this type of coaching behavior modeled by professional coaches who get red in the face and throw tantrums on the sidelines. The difference is that those pros are coaching adults, who presumably know enough to protect themselves against the mental and emotional abuse.

Our children can't protect themselves. It's up to us—conscious and empowered sports parents—to do that for them.

On the other hand, I also have had the privilege of seeing some really excellent examples of coaching. These are the men and women who strive to instill the love of the game in their players, who make the season a positive one, who understand that the youth sports experience is about so much more than the score at the end of the game or the team standings at the end of the season.

Sports, specifically team sports, provide a unique opportunity for children to learn important life lessons. Consider these opinions ...

"The values learned on the playing field—how to set goals, endure, take criticism and risks, become team players, use our beliefs, stay healthy, and deal with stress—prepare us for life."
—Donna de Varona, former American swimmer and Olympic gold-medalist

"Sports knows no sex, age, race or religion. Sports gives us all the ability to test ourselves mentally, physically and emotionally in a way no other aspect of life can. For many of us who struggle with 'fitting in' or our identity,

sports gives us our first face of confidence. That first bit of confidence can be a gateway to many other great things!"
—Dan O'Brien, former American decathlete and Olympic gold-medalist

"Sports can do so much. They've given me a framework: meeting new people, confidence, self-esteem, discipline, motivation. All these things I learned, whether I knew I was learning them or not, through sports."
—Mia Hamm, retired American soccer player and Olympic gold-medalist

Obviously, sports have more to offer our children than the trophies that collect dust and tarnish over time. These Olympians got more from their sport than their shiny gold medals.

So if sports can be so valuable to our children, why don't more parents claim their own power as their children's first—and perhaps best—coach, cheerleader, and fan?

I don't know the answer. I'm just trying to encourage more of us to do so.

We've all seen the child who is not very excited to be on the field/court/track, who doesn't love the sport he or she is playing, and who is there only in an attempt to please or get approval from a parent. These players are easy to spot by their body language—head down, no spring in the step, shoulders slumped.

He's usually the last one to take his place out on the field. She goes through the motions but never puts any real effort behind her actions. He's timid and unsure of his abilities. She's devastated by a setback or a loss. He's indifferent to the outcome of the game, the end result of a project . . . perhaps life in general.

These kids break my heart.

I would love to see *every* child be the one who walks onto the field (or into a room) with an easy confidence. She looks people in the eye and smiles often. He always gives his very best effort—in a game and at practice, in the classroom, in the community . . . in life.

She is confident of her abilities without being boastful or dominating. He is generous in his kindness to others and encourages his teammates and those around him. She doesn't let failure or a loss define her.

He knows his own strengths and weaknesses, and he makes decisions based on an awareness of his true abilities. She cares about the outcome of the game, of the school project, and of her life. He celebrates even small victories (like a fist-pump after a perfectly placed pitch).

Our children *do* learn lessons from sports. It's up to us to make sure they're learning the right ones.

Often, the positive lessons that can be learned from sports are buried beneath the ultracompetitive nature and drive of some coaches and parents. Most youth sports league coaches *are* parents. They're volunteers. But they still must be held to the highest of standards because they're helping to shape our most precious resource—our children.

Coaches have told me stories about kids for whom a sport has been their salvation—keeping them out of trouble and giving them a direction. They know these stories from firsthand experience because the stories are their own stories. They were the young athletes whose coaches meant the world to them.

Our children won't always have the ideal coach. That's reality. And that is a learning experience in and of itself. We parents need to be present and watch from the sidelines with our eyes wide open so that we can help our children understand and appreciate the differences among coaches.

We need to take each experience that comes our child's way and make even the ugly choices made by certain adults into positive learning experiences. At the very least, we need to help our athletes come to terms with—and to accept—a particular coach's limitations. We do this, of course, always with the respect that he or she *is* the coach, but also with the understanding that a coach is a person, too, just like the rest of us.

Coaches are a human being who can be wrong and who can make bad choices. This doesn't make them bad, just people who are struggling with their own issues. As conscious sports parents, we need to discuss this with our young athletes. We must talk about what appropriate behavior looks like—and what is inappropriate behavior—so that our children can judge for themselves which category their coach or any other team parent falls into.

We want our children to be good sports, good citizens. But to get them there, we parents need to get in the game and make a difference, too. We need to let the organizers, coordinators, and boards of youth sports leagues know that we will not accept coaches who exhibit inappropriate and unsportsmanlike conduct. At the same time, we need to celebrate the coaches—both paid and volunteer—who *are* doing the right things.

We need to celebrate them, thank them, and let them know that we acknowledge and appreciate them. Just as we don't want our young athletes to slip through the cracks of society, neither do we want to let these coaches fade away or get burned out.

I am so very proud of my own young athlete (he's the one who fist-pumps to celebrate the perfectly placed pitch) and his accomplishments. And I'm proud to claim my power as a sports mom. I'm sharing some of the life lessons learned from sports on the *Sports Mom Café* page. I hope you'll stop by often.

Michele Peterson is a professional writer, successful businesswoman, speaker and mom. She actively supports several community organizations and causes. She currently serves as a Director of the Fresno County Women's Chamber of Commerce, and she is President of her local chapter of BNI (Business Network International). Additionally, she is a past PTA President and still serves on the executive board of the PTA at her son's school.

She has been a soccer mom, baseball mom, football mom, and basketball mom. As her son has developed an affinity and love for baseball, she recently has transitioned into a year-round baseball mom.

Michele's *Sports Mom Café* fan page and website are intended to be resources of support, inspiration and empowerment for other sports moms, dads, grandparents, and coaches. She hopes to remind other conscious sports parents that they are not alone and that everyone can make a difference ... even if that difference in in the life of just one child on just one team.

www.facebook.com/SportsMomCafe
www.SportsMomCafe.com

Chapter Eight

Meet Chris Castillo of *Firewithin*™

Never Lose Faith. Never Lose Hope. Never Lose that Firewithin™.

My mom and I were poor, second-class citizens, without a home. We didn't have a house to call our own, so we lived in various places throughout our hometown of Antofagasta, Chile.

Like many single mothers living in Chilean society in the seventies, she was looked down on by society because she was a single mother. Society at that time regarded single mothers as second-class citizens who were not given many opportunities. A single mother was considered a disgrace to society, and therefore many opportunities were closed for us. This was the case for many single mothers living in Chile at that time.

In 1973, Chile came under military rule by Augusto Pinochet. Pinochet had ousted the socialist Allende government that had ruled Chile prior to 1973. When the military came to power and governed Chile, the government ruled the country with an iron fist, and imposed curfews.

Life was definitely hard. And this created many challenges for my mother and me. With many doors closed, the only way for way my mom and me to survive was to do odd jobs and become very entrepreneurial. Whether it was selling candies, clothing, or cleaning services, we had to do whatever to survive together. During those times, jobs were scarce and we had to become entrepreneurs.

We barely had food to eat. Whenever there was food, my mom would always ensure that I was fed first, often not leaving much or any for herself. This is a true measure of a mother's love for her child.

Throughout these difficult times, there were many impactful events that happened to us. But there are two significant events that I clearly remember.

The first major event was when we were hungry and had nothing to eat. Then, an opportunity occurred when we saw a chicken running loose. This chicken was like a gift to us. So we chased it down and caught it. It was quite an ordeal at the time. Not only did we have to chase and catch the chicken, but also try to kill it. Without any knowledge of killing a chicken, we just tried to snap its neck. The chicken was still running around. So we tried to kill it with a knife. It was definitely quite an experience.

After many efforts, we successfully killed the chicken. Then we plucked its feathers and proceeded to cook and eat it. Boy, did we eat well that night! I remember feeling like royalty because of the feast we had thanks to this chicken. It was at this point that we realized that anything is possible if you put your mind to it. And never to lose faith and hope that one day, things will get better.

After thoroughly enjoying ourselves with this feast, the next day a woman was walking around asking people if anyone had seen one of her chickens that had gone missing. When the lady asked us, we said no for fear of getting into trouble. We had been starving and desperate to eat. This feeling of desperation and wanting to eat drove us to eat that chicken.

The second major event that we went through happened in an empty room where my mom and I were squatting; the room was in a house that belonged to my grandparents , who had passed away years ago. I remember the Chilean police coming in to kick us out and throw us into the streets like dogs. The police were doing their jobs, but it was painful to go through this experience of being kicked out from an empty room that we wanted to call home. The problem at that time was that since we had no money, we could not own a home.

The police came to evict us out at the request of an uncle. This uncle had done few renovations to that room and wanted to rent it out and make money even though he knew of our poor situation. Ironically, that uncle many years later was dying in the very same room. And so my mom traveled to Chile exclusively to help him to recover, giving him medicine and money for food. Mom did this out of the kindness of her heart. He thanked her and apologized for what he had done to us. She accepted and stayed with that uncle, by his side, until he finally passed away.

And so we struggled and moved around from place to place.

But throughout these challenges, we never lost faith and hope, we always kept that fire within burning with the hope that one day things would get better for us.

And that better day came when my mother met Nelson, who was to become my stepfather. This changed things for the better for me and my mom. They fell in love with each other and he took me in as one of his own sons. I am forever grateful to him for accepting me as his own son.

My stepfather was a recent electrical engineer graduate. As a recent graduate, it was difficult to find jobs in Chile. Jobs were scarce and opportunities were limited. Then my stepfather made a critical decision that would change our lives forever. He applied to the Canadian embassy for a work visa. They told him that in Winnipeg, Manitoba, there were plenty of jobs for electrical engineers like him.

So he applied and got the opportunity to go to Winnipeg to look for a job in engineering. He took that leap of faith, scraped up enough money for an airline ticket, took what little clothing he had with him, and flew to Canada.

On arriving at the Winnipeg airport, the customs officer took his official papers, stamped them, and said "welcome to Canada." My stepfather grabbed his suitcase and proceeded to walk out of the airport. With only $300 in his pocket, not knowing anyone in Canada, not having any place to go, and only knowing very few English words, he felt ready to take on the opportunities available to him in Canada.

Then, while standing outside the airport gazing out in to the new world wondering what else to do, he remembered about a favor that his friend from Chile had asked him to do. The favor was to deliver a letter to someone in Winnipeg.

So my stepfather pulled out the letter, flagged down a taxi, and then pointed to the letter's mailing address indicating where he wanted the taxi driver to take him. The taxi driver understood and drove him to the address on the letter.

Once the taxi driver dropped him off at the address on the letter, he stepped out of the cab and then walked up to the house and knocked on the door. A Spanish-speaking man opened the door. My stepfather introduced himself, and then my stepfather told him that he was there to drop off a letter as a favor for a friend in Chile.

The man thanked him for dropping off the letter.

Then my stepfather said bye and started to walk away from the house. The man in the house asked where he was going. My stepfather said, "I'm not sure. Maybe find a church or some shelter for the night." Seeing that my stepfather had no place to go and that he was looking tired and hungry, the man invited my stepfather to stay with him until he was able to find a more permanent place to stay. It was an opportunity at a critical time of need.

One year later, my stepfather had gotten himself settled and had landed a job as a technician. He had saved enough money to pay for an airline ticket to bring me, my mom, and my baby brother, Sergio, to Canada. And this too changed our lives forever as we were brought to the amazing country of Canada.

Throughout this time, I never forgot how important it was for us not to lose faith and hope for a better day. And how important it is to keep that fire that is within us burning brightly. For it is this fire burning within each of us that keeps us motivated and keeps us going throughout difficult times. And when this fire within is coupled with faith and hope, it becomes a powerful combination for living life.

"Firewithin" is about keeping that eternal spirit within us, alive and joyous. It is about having a profound appreciation for life and realizing that one day things will be better.

And throughout my life's journey, I've always kept that fire within burning and I always remember to live life to the fullest. It is about never losing that zest for life that people have when they live life to the fullest, no matter what the circumstances or challenges we face.

We all have stories to tell about the fire that resides within us. We need to keep it alive. We need to let it burn brightly as we go through the challenges of life. We must always remember to rekindle it when we are feeling down or facing insurmountable obstacles.

Oh, and what became of that house we were kicked out of? When the police kicked us out of that empty room onto the streets? Well, as of December 2012, we are now in the final stages of acquiring it along with the whole property, and then plan to resell it. It is an opportune time as it is valued real estate, located downtown in the booming mining town of Antofagasta.

Interesting how life has twists and turns. Who would have thought that one day we would be able to own not only the room but the whole house that we were kicked out of?

In Spanish, there is a saying, "el mundo tienes muchas vueltas." It means that what goes around, comes around. It also means that be careful not to judge since one day you might be in that same situation. And finally, this also means that life has many twists and turns. And throughout the twists and turns that life throws at you, it is ever so important that we never lose faith and hope, and always try to keep that fire that is deep in us, burning brightly.

 Chris Castillo is on a mission; to *inspire, empower,* and *motivate* others to live life with passion and purpose using their unique talents. And he is an example of this! Born in Antofagasta, Chile, he lived in poverty, was homeless with his mother, and didn't know where the next meal would come from. Always on survival mode, success seemed so far away.

While in Chile, he developed the ability to "create something from nothing." This ability requires a specific mindset for identifying opportunities and mobilizing limited resources to take advantage of the opportunities.

He also developed the ability to create value, how to develop and nurture relationships, deal with people, identify and take action on business ideas, and achieve strategic leverage.

It is these experiences that have helped to shape Chris's mission; it is these experiences that have made him determined to live life passionately; it is these experiences that have made him successful.

And now he works to inspire, empower and motivate others through Firewithin™ facebook page. Chris is also a published author, entrepreneur, educator, and investor.

http://www.facebook.com/pages/Firewithin
www.chris-castillo.com

Chapter 9

Meet Chantelle Ashworth of *Where Angels and Lightworkers Meet*

"If you want a love message to be heard, it has got to be sent out. To keep a lamp burning, we have to keep putting oil in it."
—Mother Teresa

I HAVE ALWAYS FELT drawn to helping where I can and to be of service to others. Even as a child I felt that I could make a difference. I grew up in a home where both parents were always willing to go the extra mile to help other people and it was through them that I learned to give unselfishly and to love unconditionally. At one time my mother worked at a small school for mentally disabled children and my parents took in three boys who needed fostering, one of whom has been with us ever since. I often thought of my mother as a modern-day saint and I remember feeling a strong desire to be just like my mom when I grew up. I sometimes felt like it wasn't normal to want to help others as much as I did and I didn't want anyone questioning my motives, when I didn't even know what they were myself. It was only later in life that I realized that I was not the only one and this is how I came to learn of Lightworkers.

I did end up following in my mother's footsteps, and studied to be a preschool teacher. Now here was somewhere I could make a positive contribution on a daily basis. While still a student I volunteered at an impoverished school in a shanty township where there were no running water or toilet facilities and the classroom floor was a dirt floor with a shabby carpet thrown over it. I used to tell anyone who would listen that my dream job one day would be to teach in a school just like that.

As it turns out, ten years later, I was offered my dream job and I jumped at the opportunity to be of real service to my fellow man. Little did I know that I was about to embark on the journey of a lifetime. These children, and their families, lived in tin shacks with no running water or electricity. Most of them were HIV-positive or had someone in their family who was. Being a part of all this really touched my heart and gave me an even stronger sense of gratitude for all that I had.

Many things happened at this stage in my life, but three things stand out the most and would change the course of my life forever. After years of telling myself that I didn't want to be a statistic, I finally found the courage to divorce my husband of ten years. I learned that I was strong enough to survive almost anything and and to not have any regrets in life. A few months later I bumped into an old childhood friend and we rekindled our friendship. He became my life coach, and I found myself experiencing a remarkable transformation and awakening. It's funny how life's greatest trials teach us the most about ourselves and who we are in the greater scheme of things. I first heard of vision boards from an Oprah show and then after seeing it on *The Secret,* I decided to give it a go. "Let me see how this manifesting thing really works," I thought. I funnily enough had been collecting little phrases and pictures of things that resonated with me since I was in high school, so I pulled that out of the bottom draw of my desk and spread it all out on the floor. One of the things that jumped out at me was a picture of an apple on a pile of books with a quote about "giving a teacher an apple." I looked at this for a long time and after lots of thought and deliberation, I decided it would not go on my vision board, the main reason being the children at the school were all receiving food parcels to help feed their families, and they very rarely saw fresh fruit anyway. I doubted that I would ever be the recipient of this very precious commodity. I spent the next hour or so designing my vision board and then went to bed. I will never forget the surprise I got when I arrived at school the next day. I had just sat down at my desk when one of the little girls in my class came up to me and handed me a bright, red apple. I was speechless! I had to ask her several times if the apple really was for me. Needless to say, I had never received such a sweet gift before in my life.

That night I sat up for hours, cutting up magazines and very carefully selecting what I wanted on my vision board. I was 34 years old and divorced with two beautiful daughters to think about. I was going to do this the right way!

Even after the upset of divorce, I never gave up on love. One of the first pictures I looked for was one of a suitable man. I ended up using a picture from an article on *The Amazing Race*. I remembered the guy in the article. He was not caught up in all the drama of the race and just enjoyed living in the moment—my kind of guy. The article mentioned that he was 28 years old, which made me doubt my choice of picture just a little bit. The experts will tell you to be very specific when putting something on your vision board because what you see is what you'll get. I stuck it on there anyway! It was about three months later that I met this really sweet man, we fell in love, and got married.

He was 28 years old.

I have always believed that everything happens for a reason and that something good will always come from it, so I was not surprised when things started turning around for me. I learned the power of positive thinking, manifestation, and having an attitude of gratitude and from that I met my second husband, bought my first home, and was living a joyful life.

It was at this time in my life that I joined Facebook and I found myself learning things that I never thought possible. It was here that I found daily encouragement and motivation to be the me I was destined to be. It was here I learned about Lightworkers.

I had a very strong calling to share all this wonderful new knowledge with others and in some way help them to overcome limiting beliefs and fears that may be holding them back. Not everybody has a best friend and life coach all rolled into one to help them when life is trying to teach them something new. Realistically, I knew that I could not be that person for everyone I met. So with a strong calling to share what I knew with others, it didn't take long for me to realize the power of Facebook and the number of people I could reach. I could share with like-minded people and hopefully help them grow as individuals and at the same time get some spiritual uplifting myself. This was the start of Where Angels and Lightworkers Meet.

Every day I am grateful that I have this platform from which to reach the world and all the beautiful people in it. I learn as much from the people on Where Angels and Lightworkers Meet as I hope they learn from me, and to be able to share with them my beliefs, my fears, and my truths has been an unexpected but wonderful blessing.

My husband and I may not always have the same beliefs or opinions but he has always believed in me and has now encouraged and motivated me to start a website whereby I may reach even more people. I would love for the website Where Angels and Lightworkers Meet to become a source of inspiration to those who need it, motivation for those of us who need a little push in life, and a place for people to find their true selves. I value the opinions of others and would welcome any comments or feedback given.

I want the love message to be heard. I am sending it out.

 As life dishes out its lessons, some choose to ignore them and others choose to use them for the greater good. Chantelle has chosen to use her life's lessons for the greater good and thus believes wholeheartedly in the abilities of others. Empowering and inspiring others to be true to themselves has become Chantelle's daily mission. Where Angels and Lightworkers Meet and Parenting Our Precious Gifts

(inspired by her miracle baby boy) are two Facebook pages that Chantelle uses to achieve just that.

Chantelle was born in Harare, Zimbabwe, and then relocated with her family to Port Elizabeth, South Africa, at the age of 6. Graduating from Alexander Road High School and doing a year of extra studies in criminology, ethnology, physiology and history aided her in achieving her dream to be a preschool teacher. She studied preschool (kindergarten) teaching at the CTCE (Cape Town College of Education). During her thirteen years as a teacher, Chantelle fulfilled a lifelong dream to work with underprivileged children and their families.

She has also worked as an occupational therapist assistant in a rehabilitation hospital. During this period Chantelle married and conceived two daughters, Jodi and Jaime. She has since then remarried, and Chantelle and her husband, Richard, conceived a son which also brought about the "birth" of Baby Liam Sebastian Ashworth the Precious Gift.

Chantelle now gives arts and crafts workshops for children at an annual initiative for young entrepreneurs, and you will often find her in her free time doing crafts and gardening. A newly acquired skill has led Chantelle to make and sell crystal healing wands from her Facebook page, Divinely Timed Crystal Wands.

Where Angels and Lightworkers Meet:
https://www.facebook.com/pages/Where-Angels-and-Lightworkers-Meet

Divinely Timed Crystal Creations:
https://www.facebook.com/pages/Divinely-Timed-Crystal-Creations

Parenting Our Precious Gifts:
https://www.facebook.com/ParentingOurPreciousGifts

Baby Liam Sebastian Ashworth the precious gift:
*https://www.facebook.com/
BabyLiamSebastianAshworthThePreciousGift*

Some of the thanks received from people on
Where Angels and Lightworkers Meet:

"Thank you so much again. You have shown your compassion and loving side. This means a lot. Thank you again."

"Okay, so thank you, thank you, thank you. Your gift is beautiful, and it took a lot off stress of my mind. You helped both my son and I out more than you will ever know. In summary, listen to your hubby and the angels, as it is your calling."

"Thank you so much for your open and honest response."

"Thank you for making me feel better and I appreciate your time."

"You and your messages have been a blessing for me and I share them with my friends also. Thank you."

"Thank you Chantelle...I am going though the hardest time of my life. Literally at rock bottom in all areas. I needed this today more than you can know."

"You're an inspiration to me and to so many others I bet!"

"Always a pleasure reading your posts and resonating with your pages too!"

"Keep posting those wonderful posts and spreading your contagious positive attitude."

"Have you any idea how much this message means to me? It changed my whole outlook and I want to thank you from the bottom of my heart for staying true to yourself and for telling the Truth! You are an amazing Being

and I am so very honored to know you. I know the Angels brought you to my Path especially for this day."

"You are always so positive, kind and attentive to your 'friends', their feelings and emotions. You are a true angel on earth for so many of us. I am very grateful and thrilled that you have crossed my path therefore truly enhancing it and gracing it with your presence. "

"Hello Chantelle... I love your page. I am inspired by the things you post. Thank you for shining your inner Light to share."

Chapter 10

Meet Sherryl Frauenglass: *A Woman's True Voice*

Redefining Normal

THE MOMENT I DISCOVERED I was pregnant, I knew that the child I was carrying was going to change my life forever. Of course this is how almost every mother feels, and it's true that children always change our lives significantly, but looking back on that moment, I knew that my baby was going to have a profound impact on my life and the lives of everyone he came in contact with. Little did I know that he was destined to shake the very foundation of my belief system.

Chasing Normal

Growing up in a somewhat typical dysfunctional family, I always compared myself with other people and measuring how my family life stacked up against theirs. I desperately wanted to be "normal" and fit in. I tried for years to fix whatever I perceived was wrong with me, and was always looking outside of myself for validation and confirmation that I was okay. Since nothing I tried seemed to change anything, I decided to create a "normal" family myself. If I could just find a man, have a couple of kids and a nice house, then maybe I would be like everyone else.

I met my former husband when I was 26 and within a few days he told me that he would love to have a baby with me. I was sure that he was kidding, but in the back of my mind I thought I had found my ticket to a seat on the "normal" train. When I became pregnant six months later, I was sure that my future was secure.

Unfortunately, there was nothing about my life that was in any way "normal." We moved to a remote town in northern New England, which was a shock for someone raised in the suburbs. It became clear fairly quickly that marrying someone because you wanted to have a baby was not a good basis for a relationship. We struggled with our differences right from the beginning.

My beautiful son was born at home with two wonderful midwives to assist. After 42 hours of slow labor, he was born blue and not breathing. The midwives were quickly able to revive him, but that minute seemed like hours as his father and I prayed and rubbed his tiny feet, telling him that we really wanted him to be here. I've looked back at that moment many times and now believe that he was having second thoughts about coming into this life. He knew that it was not going to be an easy journey and he wanted to make sure that we really wanted to go through it with him.

Jason* was a bright and sensitive child. He was quite empathic from an early age, but other than that, and much to my relief, he seemed totally normal. As he got older, his sensitive nature became more of a challenge as he tried to deal with the instability in our home and in the world. When he was just 12 years old, he began to secretly use marijuana to cope with the stress and challenges that come with onset of puberty.

Any "unusual" behaviors or signs that might have appeared up until this point, I attributed to him being a typical teenager or to his pot smoking. When Jason turned 16, he began to challenge his father, which made their relationship even more difficult. The troubles in my marriage also accelerated, and this time and my husband and I separated and eventually divorced. I thought this would normalize our home environment and take some of the stress away from Jason, but his drug use seemed to accelerate and I eventually kicked him out for having marijuana in my home. He lived with his father for a while and then eventually got a job and shared a house with his best friend. He seemed to be turning his life around and had decided to enroll in the School of Integrative Nutrition in NYC. He had a natural affinity for nutrition and health and had cured himself of years of bad acne simply by applying his encyclopedic knowledge of nutrition and nutraceuticals.

Normal Hits the Road

Everything shifted the summer before Jason was supposed to go away to school. One day late in June, he appeared at my house very agitated and confused. He wanted to leave his car in my driveway and kept shoving a nutritional company brochure in my face. He was pointing at the text in the brochure and explaining to me how there was a government conspiracy associated with the things printed there. He was mixing up words and making associations that didn't make any sense. I knew that something was terribly wrong but wasn't sure what to do. Fairly quickly I realized that I needed to call an ambulance and get him to the hospital. I left him standing in the driveway for just a couple of minutes while I went inside to get my phone, but by the time I returned, he had disappeared. I panicked!

I spent the next three days driving around town, calling all of his friends and family members, but no one had heard from him. His roommate said that he had noticed Jason acting a little odd and paranoid over the past week but wasn't sure what to do about it.

Finally, after an agonizing few days, on the Fourth of July I received a telephone call from a senior assisted living facility 400 miles away. They had found Jason wandering around in a field next to their facility, and knew there was something wrong and had already called an ambulance. They gave me the phone to speak to him and he happily told me that he had gone to find his true mother, Mother Earth, and that he was here to "save the Fourth of July."

This was the beginning of an emotional roller coaster ride for my entire family and me. After several hospitalizations and many psychiatric visits, Jason was officially declared SMI (Seriously Mentally Ill) with a diagnosis of schizoaffective disorder (a combination of schizophrenia and unspecified personality disorder). While I've come to realize that this label does not fit the complex being that is my son, it has granted him access to social services and medical benefits.

Redefining Normal

It may sound a bit extreme, but the only way to adequately describe what it's like having a loved one experience a psychotic break is to compare it to a death. While my son obviously didn't actually die, the part of him that I dreamed would have a "normal" life was gone forever. What really died was my picture of what normal was supposed to be. I went through years of battling the system to get him services. We tried many alternative treatments and healing modalities, but nothing brought back the son that I felt I had lost. As with any perceived loss, I went through all of the stages of grief.

Denial: How could this be happening to my kid? How could this be happening to me? It will all blow over and he will normal again soon.

Guilt: It must somehow be my fault. I should have seen the symptoms.

Anger: It must be someone else's fault. Who or what can I blame?

Bargaining: If he comes through this, I promise I'll pay more attention to him and help him get his life together.

Depression: This is hopeless. I don't know what to do. No one really understands what I'm going through.

Turning Point: I notice that he doesn't seem to be suffering with this and actually seems pretty happy. Maybe it's going to be okay.

Acceptance: This may not be the life I would have chosen for my child, but he is doing it his way.

A New Normal

After years of struggling with trying to fix him, I have come to a place of deep peace and understanding of my son's unique journey. I now know the truth about Jason and that he, like each of us, is a divine child of God/universe, here to do his part on Earth. I learned how to connect with his higher self rather than his psychosis, and whenever I energetically tuned into his true voice, I would hear things like, "Don't worry mom. I'm having a great time." Or "I actually enjoy being here in the hospital. It's fun to push the staff's buttons."

So what the heck is "normal" anyway? Sometimes the things that come out of Jason's mouth have me wondering if we're the crazy ones and he really knows the truth. The more dramatic incidences involving the police and hospital staff clearly show that he is a true freedom seeker here to cause people to question systems and policies. Often what works with other patients does not work with him, and they've had to find new ways of dealing with his psychotic episodes other than sedation and behavioral modification techniques.

In order to find peace in a situation like this, it's necessary to understand the bigger picture. We each come to earth with something unique to contribute. For some, this means that we're here to shake a few trees to get people out of their comfort zones. Whether your children functions within "normal" society or needs assistance, they are still contributing to the overall uplifting and awakening of the planet, or else they wouldn't even be here. When you realize that they're not actually broken and don't need fixing, it frees you both to get on with the business of living the life you were meant to live.

Over the years I have worked hard to set up a support network within the state system, so that my son could live as independently as possible. He still goes in and out of the hospital when he decides to stop taking his medication, but he now has a team that watches out for him so that it doesn't always fall on my shoulders. I still sometimes assist him with things like shopping or doing laundry, but I treat him as the brilliant light that he is.

When I share my story or describe the latest incident with my son, and a concerned, sympathetic look comes over the listeners' faces, I remind them that Jason is actually happier than just about anyone I know. Perhaps "normal" is overrated?

*Name has been changed to protect my son's privacy

 Sherryl Frauenglass is an awakening coach, visionary entrepreneur, and inspirational speaker, who loves to co-create at the leading edge of change. Sherryl assists people with change-the-world missions, to connect with their true voice and then effectively transmit their message out to the world.

Sherryl also has a deep passion for assisting parents, as well as other family members, of children with mental health challenges. Through her compassionate heart, personal experience, and spiritual perspective, she helps her clients come to a place of peace and understanding of their child's journey. She offers live and virtual classes, one-on-one coaching and mentoring to those who are ready to soar!

www.TrueVoiceCommunications.com
www.facebook.com/AWomansTrueVoice
www.facebook.com/WideAwakeNetwork
http://www.facebook.com/ByeByeNormal
http://www.facebook.com/FeedingTheGoddess

Chapter 11

Meet Justin Nutt: *The Good Guy, The Bad Guy, and The Ugly Truth*

PASSION AND INSPIRATION can come from a number of places, and often from more than one source. And for me, this is most definitely the case. My passion for each page and endeavor may have come from a specific event, but the fruition of those endeavors come from a culmination of my life experiences. It is for this reason that all that is in my past—the good, the bad, and the ugly—are all things that I fully embrace. Henry Ford said, "Failure is the only opportunity to begin again more intelligently," and it is no different with life experiences; each moment, be it good or bad, in turn makes you the person you are. While at times the progression of a person's passion is linear, many times instead they exist through seemingly unrelated events that, when added together, create something that is much greater than simply the sum of the parts. My story is much more the latter than the former.

For me, the first element that led me to the point I am at now was a series of bad relationships after having grown up in what could largely be compared to a *Leave it to Beaver* childhood. In my first relationship, true relationship, I was in love from the first moment we kissed. However, we were not meant to be because of aspects of her life: She was separated from her husband and she ended up going back to him. There was no explanation, no good-bye, she was just gone one day and I never knew why. I was forced to question what I had done wrong and what I could do better the next time. I didn't want to turn to anyone, didn't want to ask for help, because that would mean admitting what had happened. This had an effect on me as it does every guy who gets a "Dear John" letter, or, as in my case, no letter at all.

My next relationship was with a woman I loved but wasn't truly in love with. We ended up getting married, I've since realized, simply because I didn't want to be alone. This of course didn't work and led to me leaving after a mere ten months and twenty-eight days. I must admit that I wasn't the best of men with her. Having grown up with parents who loved and respected each other, when I was presented with a relationship that was abusive (even getting in a fight on our wedding night and sleeping apart), I knew not what to do. The more we argued and the more she treated me badly, the more I grew to resent her. Our marriage grew into a battle to try and hurt the other first. I always assumed this was her fault, and in part it was, but it was also the result of previous relationships that hadn't worked out, for me and for her.

Then there was a girl whom I had a crush on in high school; it was a rather whirlwind experience and not really in a good way. She too was married, but we were infatuated with each other. Since she was planning to leave him anyway, we began dating, but this too was short-lived. Her experience from dating bad guys and marrying one had made her desire to be the nurturer, and as a social worker and with my bad experiences, I was used to doing that. It ended badly because of this fact, and yet again I was forced to question myself. I knew that I hadn't liked how I was with my ex-wife, so I have resolved never to be that way again. With her, I tried to meet her every need and extend myself to limits I never would have previously. When it ended, I ran through a series of pseudorelationships, which led to me giving up. I thought to myself, screw it, no one is going to want me, and it's pointless to keep trying.

Then came a girl who was unlike any other, I loved her on a level that I never thought possible. I could have spent a lifetime just staring into her eyes. That too, though, as you may be able to tell by the use of past tense, ended. I had tried so hard, harder than I had in any previous relationship, with her and still I heard the "you are who I should be with, but I don't feel that spark." That devastated me, and I fought and fought to stay friends with her, but every time we kissed or had sex it was all brought back to me. She would often say that we shouldn't do those things because of how I felt; I would lie to her and myself and say that I was over her, but I never was. I always thought that if I loved her just a little bit more, if I tried just a little bit harder, that I could make her see that I was worthy of her love. This relationship taught me more in the eight months that I knew her than I will probably learn from any other: In math 2+0 and 1+1 may equal the same thing, but in love it most assuredly *does not*!

The writing of my first book, *The Good Guy, the Bad Guy, and the Ugly Truth,* which was designed to help others with patterns of unhealthy relationships, was actually the source of my own healing, at least in part. I had one last bad relationship but realized the flawed thinking, and when it ended, I worried not about finding a new relationship. Once I got to the point where I had dealt with the past and loved myself regardless of anyone else's feelings for me, I was ready for a healthy relationship, but I wasn't worried about having one. I did find one with Shannon, the woman who will soon be my wife.

After a few months with Shannon, the Joplin tornado happened. I was with a friend, and we watched as events unfolded. I woke up early the next morning knowing I had to help, and went home and started a Facebook page to aid in relief. The page exploded and a news story was written on all of our efforts. With the huge outpouring of a desire from strangers to help, I knew it could be greater than I had envisioned. I founded Acts of Random Kindness (ARK) and it took off from there. I helped as much as I could with the Texas wildfires, but with finishing my master's, I didn't accomplish a great deal.

ARK sat on the back burner until I had finished my master's, but that was another step toward my destiny. As a part of working toward my master's degree, I created Changing Patterns to help clients with healing from unhealthy relationships and I was amazed with the outcome of the program. While it was based on my own experiences, it seemed to fit so many others perfectly. The members of the group went from blaming themselves and hating who they were to accepting themselves, loving themselves no matter what the outside world thought of them. When I went over the post tests that showed the improvements, I thought it wasn't possible. I sat down with each one and when we talked in private sessions, I could see that these were the true results, and that the members did not just desire to please me.

It was at this point that I again saw that possibility. The project was for a grade, but the outcomes were my focus and they were real. I actually only cared about the grade because of the huge change that occurred for the participants. The project no longer was mine; it was something bigger than me. On June 6, 2012, I decided ARK needed to become more: It wasn't just passion, it was about obligation, too. As such, ARK shifted purposes: No longer was it about natural disasters, which occur occasionally, but the greater issues of healing, of which there are so many more. I blended my past, my passions, and my successes and ARK started working toward implementing Changing Patterns in domestic violence shelters, in part because I was some people who worked in shelters reached out to me.

I began to write a new book, which is still in the works, that dealt with similar issues as my first which was broadened to deal not only with romantic relationships but with how so many people who enter our lives affect our self-worth. Each time I had an epiphany while driving or eating, or awoke with one in my head, I would write it down (or text it to myself). I often blended these with pictures that fit the thought and began to post them. At the same time, I began talking with survivors of domestic violence and they would ask to share these pictures on their own pages, or I would want to share the pictures and would do so on their pages. I talked with one administrator of a page and she suggested tagging them on other pages. I did that one time with one picture, and there was an explosion. Where before there had been one or two notifications in the morning, it began to rise to twenty-plus and hundreds of shares and likes on a picture. People would message the page and thank me, and tell me how alone they felt but that they now saw hope since others had been there and come out better for the experience. This only deepened my passion, my inspiration, and my desire to help and to post pictures. Where I once created a quote picture once a week or so, I now am inspired to create one each day, and write that much more. And yes, while it is I who write them, they don't belong to me; they belong to everyone.

This is the power of Facebook, the power to connect people, and the most ironic part is that at one point I was the person who swore he would never have a Facebook. The reach of my passion now extends far beyond those I can interact with on a one-on-one basis to now making this passion available to people from all around the world. Asia, Africa, Europe, South America, every continent has a fan on my page who has been touched by my passion, who as a result has touched me on many levels and most certainly increased my passion that much more. It is amazing that you can have a passion for anything and through Facebook fan pages more easily reach those for whom it will resonate. And the inspiration goes both ways, for both myself and for whom it can impact and change their life for the better.

 Justin Nutt, a dating and relationship expert, is a therapist currently working in the Kansas City area with a specialty in relationship counseling and identity issues connected to self-esteem and self-worth. In November 2012, ARK Counseling Services was opened by Justin and his fiancée, Shannon, in Paola, Kansas, to provide mental health services to those in Miami, Linn, Franklin, and Anderson Counties, Kansas. Justin holds an undergraduate degree in social work from the University of Kansas and a Master of Social Work from the University of Missouri: Kansas City. Justin is currently a member of the Kansas and National chapters of the NASW (National Association for Social Workers).

Justin is also the founder and executive director of Acts of Random Kindness (ARK), a disaster relief organization created in May of 2011 to help connect individuals and families with temporary and permanent housing, needed relief supplies, and food, in the wake of natural disasters. As of June 4, 2012, Acts of Random Kindness began working to provide relief to the victims of domestic violence and is working to partner with domestic violence shelters across the United States to begin implementation of the Changing Patterns program, which is based on Justin's book *The Good Guy, the Bad Guy, and the Ugly Truth,* as a part of treatment in shelters. All proceeds from sales of *The Good Guy, the Bad Guy, and the Ugly Truth,* as well as other products or services purchased through his website are used to fund the domestic violence work of Acts of Random Kindness.

Justin's published works include poetry magazines; his first relationship therapy book, *The Good Guy, the Bad Guy, and the Ugly Truth*; and a special issue of the *Journal of Evidenced Based Social Work.* Justin also is in the process of publishing a children's book and a book on the history of Christmas traditions. He is also currently working on eight new works, which are in various stages of development, with topics ranging from therapy to a crime novel. Justin is also working with a director and producer to film one of his screenplays.

https://www.facebook.com/Acts.Random.Kindness
https://www.facebook.com/GoodGuy.BadGuy.UglyTruth
https://www.facebook.com/pages/ARK-Counseling-Services
https://www.facebook.com/HistoryofChristmas

Chapter 12

Meet Sally Fisher

The Inspiration of AIDS

I WAS WORKING AT The Actor's Institute in New York when friends, colleagues, and students started showing strange, seemingly unrelated symptoms, of what, we didn't yet know. But it appeared to happen primarily among gay men, one of whom, Max Navar, was my acting student, pal, and an early AIDS patient and activist. As his face became drawn, he began to lobby me to organize a support group for the people around the institute who were impacted by this new life-threatening presence. Dan Fauci, the founder and director of the institute, offered us space there. The group grew and grew, and one day Max began to lobby me again. No, that's wrong. His requests ran the gamut from lobby to beg, to demand, to pressure to flatter me into doing a workshop specifically for people with AIDS, which had shown up among those in the arts early in the epidemic. Of course I agreed.

It was a challenge, which is something I have trouble resisting, but more importantly, it was something that I could actually do for my lovely friends whose lives were being threatened. I created the centerpiece of the workshop from my own spiritually based workshops. I borrowed pieces of Dan's *Mastery of Acting* and included an array of psychological principles, emotional exercises, and information about transmission pathways, safe sex, relationships, and death. I called the workshop the AIDS Mastery, because it occurred to me that, like acting, where you could master the art of living fully while practicing your craft even if you had no control over getting hired, getting great reviews, or becoming famous, AIDS was about living your life fully and making it an adventure even though you had no idea if you were going to live for sixty years or die from AIDS-related infections in six months or six years. Again, Dan offered us space at the institute for the workshop.

I have a philosophy that I deeply believe and return to whenever things seem impossible, in order to persevere: The quality of life is not determined by the circumstances, but by how we hold them and what we do with them. My acting and women's workshops usually provided the perfect place to introduce that concept. But the Friday evening of that first AIDS Mastery, as I watched my wonderful group of volunteers welcome the participants, I had doubts. I panicked. Though HIV-negative men who worked in the movement or supported their friends with AIDS, and HIV-positive men with no sign of illness were showing up, there were also others who struggled to walk. A few were wasting away; several had the skin lesions of Kaposi's sarcoma, two were in wheelchairs, one was on a gurney. Among the group of twenty men, one was accompanied by a nurse who changed his IV bags. I hadn't really counted on so many people being so ill. I sought refuge in the quiet of the office, sat down at my desk, and buried my face in my hands for a few minutes. Some of the guys were in a lot worse shape than most of the men in my support group, some of whom were also in attendance. I wondered how the quality of their lives could not be determined by the horrible circumstances of their disease.

When I pulled myself up and went back out to join the preworkshop group, the nurse approached me and said, "Look, I have to be here all weekend. Can I take the workshop along with the guys?" Her participation made me realize that the work could also serve everyone involved in what we called the AIDS community. The workshops began on Friday evening and ran all day and evening on Saturday and Sunday. I began this first Friday evening by introducing myself, telling my story and how I got involved with AIDS. Then all of the assistants who had greeted, invited, and would prepare meals for the participants during the weekend briefly introduced themselves. By that time the ice was broken and so we took our first break. The participants chatted with one another and the assistants until they were called back into the course room. It was time for each of them to go up to the front of the room, or speak from their gurney, and tell the assemblage about themselves, their relationship to HIV/AIDS, and what they wanted from the workshop. They were so courageous, totally present, and engaged with each of the other participants' stories and needs that I was thrilled. As the workshop progressed I relaxed and realized they had all come to make whatever their journey with HIV/AIDS was as good as it could possibly be given their circumstances.

At the end of the weekend I asked each participant says whatever they needed to in order to complete the workshop for themselves. After that we had a celebration during which two of the group of Actors Institute people who helped me set up and enroll the workshop, Chuck Baier and Victor Phillips, lovers for eleven years at that time, came up to me and asked if they could be my partners and make sure the workshops took place all over the country. The thing I had forgotten about this couple was that they met while training to work with Maharishi Mahesh Yogi. The next day when they brought me a map of where we might hold workshops, it was covered with red dots. They took on the task of forming the infrastructure to produce workshops and to set them up. I resigned my position at the institute because I seemed compelled to do this new work. Dan Fauci and my son, Fisher Stevens, who was then a young actor, threw a celebrity fundraiser at the institute for us.

Chuck, Victor, and I founded Northern Lights Alternatives to produce the workshops, and I began a new phase of my life called "On the Road."

I had a thought that showed up about once a day for the next week, "What was I thinking?" But there was a lot to do before we could actually begin, the first of which was to turn Northern Lights into a nonprofit organization. Next, while Chuck and Victor did that and made arrangements in cities represented by those dots and in cities where there were Actors Institutes, I went to London to do the first U.K. AIDS Masteries which I'd already set up, and then flew to Los Angeles to do another I'd arranged. After that, my next job appeared to me. It was simple; to surrender to the mystery of not knowing where this turn of my life might take me. We estimated that it would take a few years at most for researchers and doctors to get to the root of the antivirus that was taking away our loved ones. After all, it hadn't taken long to find the cause and cure for *Legionnaires' disease*. What I hadn't counted on was how wrong that theory would turn out to be. The other thing I hadn't counted on was just how miraculous the adventure I was embarking on would turn out to be.

I had been planning to move to London but committing to Northern Lights Alternatives made that impossible. I would do workshops in the United Kingdom every few months, but live in Los Angeles while Chuck and Victor held down New York, which still felt like home to me and in fact is my current home. Travel became my lifestyle. The work kept expanding because someone from Virginia who did the workshop in one city would invite us to take the work to their home city. A woman from Dallas and a man from Houston did a workshop in Santa Fe and took it to their cities; a woman from Leeds took the London workshop. My life became filled with amazingly moving weekends, with exhausting travel and fundraising in between. It was tiring, and I began to become a less joyous person, but it was clear that it wasn't about the illness and death that I encountered. I was constantly meeting wonderful, loving, powerful men, and then women, as the disease expanded its base, and there was something about holding someone as they left this life that felt very close to God.

I am by nature an activist and so with other leaders in the AIDS movement I participated in demonstrations in many cities, but primarily Los Angeles, San Francisco, New York, and Washington, DC, and even got arrested from time to time. I also continued widening my circle of friends everywhere and expanding the heartbreak. Chuck and Victor both died before the coming of protease inhibitors, the drugs which radically altered the face of the epidemic and have enabled many dear friends, colleagues, and others from those early days to survive to this day. At a certain point I saw that I just couldn't keep doing the workshops by myself with the help of only a few others. So I put together a training, invited a group of men and women who were already leaders in their own right to become AIDS mastery facilitators, and we spent glorious days under Santa Fe skies forming a smart, brave, and committed group to take the work across the country and move participants with their brilliant facilitation and great energy. As for me, I learned how empowering letting go can be. The work of the AIDS mastery spread to thirty cities in several countries and took on a life of its own. Currently the workshops still occur, though not as frequently nor in as many places, nor with the kind of urgency of previous years. So we are free to deal with a broad variety of issues surrounding life with HIV/AIDS, rather than focusing on the looming shadow of death.

Although I was very grateful for President George W. Bush's PEPFAR (the *President's Emergency Plan for AIDS Relief*), given my innate activism I was also free to turn my attention *to the insane, unnecessary,* challenging, and murderous post-9/11 entry into his very own war in Iraq, a country that had nothing to do with the terrible events of that day. Nothing. This was the second war that my country had been dragged into that I'd protested. I lived in Chicago when all hell broke out during the 1968 Democratic convention when Mayor Richard J. Daily sent his police to arrest peaceful supporters of Eugene McCarthy who were protesting in Grant Park across from the Hilton Hotel where the candidates were headquartered. More recently I slipped and fell while occupying Wall Street and sustained a leg injury, which has left me walking with a cane and without any comfort whatsoever about plying my politics and activism on the streets. And joy of joys, in this amazing electronic age, I've simply upped my participation online through my blog, "Don't Just Stand There. Do Something" *(www.dontjuststand. com)*, and Facebook, which allows me not just to sound off to people I would never be able to reach out to otherwise, but to learn what they think, feel, and believe.

When Chuck, Victor, and I founded Northern Lights Alternatives, we created a mission statement, "To be out of business." It had been our intention that the end of our organization would be brought about by an end to AIDS. And though we're getting closer and there are a few people who refer to the phase we are now in as the end of AIDS, until there's an actual end, we're still here and this work, and the work of speaking out about the kind of country I want to live in, goes on.

Sally Fisher is celebrity ambassador liaison, for newZonia, a new dimension of the Internet; founder and president of INTERSECT Worldwide, building coalitions to end the co-epidemics of HIV/AIDS and Violence Against Women and Girls in India and South Africa; co-founder of Northern Lights Alternatives; and creator, in 1986, of the AIDS Mastery Workshop, which is still facilitated in cities across the United States and United Kingdom. She is the author of *Life Mastery* based on that work. Sally is a presenter at International AIDS, U.S. AIDS and United Nations conferences on the links between gender-based violence and the global AIDS crisis. Her history in the theater include being a founding member of Dan Fauci's original Actors Institute and a founder of V-Day, benefiting organizations fighting violence against women. Producer of V-Day events from 1998 through 2002 at Madison Square Garden, the Apollo Theater, and co-producer at the Old Vic. She was an associate producer on *The Vagina Monologues, The Good Body,"* and has sat on the board of the Santa Fe Rape Crisis Center, Apne Aap in India, and remains active on the board of the Colin Higgins Foundation and newZonia. Fisher's new book in progress and a blog by the same name, "Don't Just Stand There. Do Something" challenges us all to take an active role in the life and politics of our country.

https://www.facebook.com/sally.fisher

Please view my Blog "Don't Just Stand There. Do Something"
http://www.dontjuststand.com

*"Never doubt that a small group of thoughtful committed citizens can
change the world. Indeed, it is the only thing that ever has."*
—Margaret Mead

Chapter 13

Meet Rev. Sandy Schwartz

The Thread That Unites Us All

*"If I had the chance to live my life over, I'd do things a
little different . . . I'd have more friends."*
—Ty Cobb

When recently asked why I started my Facebook page and what it means
to me, I have to admit that most of my initial curiosity was simply to
see what held the interest of my teenage daughter, along with so many
of her friends. I, of course, had heard about the brilliant young man,
Mark Zuckerberg, CEO of the Facebook phenomenon, but I knew very
little about it beyond that. Actually, as I first started using Facebook,
it seemed a little cumbersome to me, typing messages rather than just
picking up the phone and placing a call. However, I decided to keep
an open mind, and on January 13, 2009, I opened my first Facebook
account.

Like so many before me, I quickly discovered that having friends across the country and around the world was compelling, and I found myself checking in regularly, sharing thoughts and activities and just catching up on the lives of my many new "friends." And when I say *many* new friends, I mean exactly that! The numbers of these new friends really started to mushroom. In the beginning, I was encouraged to make Facebook friends by inviting personal friends and existing email lists. Then, I sent friend requests to family, neighbors, and business associates, many of whom responded affirmatively. Before long I noticed I, too, was receiving friend requests, which I naturally accepted. I can tell you, as an only child who always treasured her friends, making all these new ones felt like having a giant birthday party where everyone showed up! It felt so good to get so many positive responses and often with little notes of thanks included. I loved the sense of connection that was forming, and as the momentum built I invited friends of friends and others who shared similar interests. Again, the responses were swift and usually affirmative.

After a few weeks, however, I was dismayed to learn that my captivation and desire to add new friends soon overwhelmed the Facebook system guidelines and my account was frozen. Bewildered, I asked my computer-savvy daughter what might have happened. Without hesitation she said they evidently thought I was spam(and I don't mean the canned meat product) and blocked my account. After she explained to me that spam was an automated computer program that can seize control of lists and send undesirable email to its members, I went about the tedious process of getting in touch with someone at Facebook. After assuring them that I was not spam, but a real person, they reset my account. Apparently, however, my pace of adding friends was still beyond Facebook standards, so within two weeks my account was again frozen. This time I was unable to reach anyone to assist me in reversing the action, so I was forced to start my Facebook account all over with a different email address and password. Though I was very disappointed and saddened by perhaps losing some of my newly established friends, I did begin anew. This time I friended much more slowly and cautiously to prevent my second account meeting the same fate as my first. To this day that first account is still frozen, but my second account has now topped 5,000 friends, which is another Facebook limit. Now my growth has to be through subscriptions, which I understand is limitless. *Care to join me! :~)*

I realized early in my Facebook experience how good it felt to be connected, in real time, reaching across oceans and borders to share my life with old and new friends, alike. I believe one of the main reasons so many of us tune in to our timelines and pages each day is to deepen that sense of connection and sharing. Facebook, along with the other forms of social media, certainly has made the world a smaller, more accessible and friendly place. As a spiritual teacher and writer I love the fact that every time we post anything, that writing has the capacity to encircle the globe, touch and inspire countless lives, and through that ripple effect truly make a difference in our world. I find that the most compelling aspect to Facebook, indeed the one that drew me in, held my attention, and won my respect.

How about you? What attracted you to Facebook? Have you ever wondered what it is about the Facebook phenomenon that has propelled it to become so popular? I hear it's now a billion strong and growing. I would like to suggest that perhaps Facebook's immense popularity is because it helps us emulate a connection we already intuit to be true, that we are already connected at the soul level. We are one human family, and it really does matter what happens to our brothers and sisters across the ocean—as it happens to us, also. We are innately interested in and of importance to one another. Facebook provides a platform for many of us to live in that connection.

In addition, it is my hope that Facebook, along with the other forms of social media, through facilitating this open and direct communication, will steadily lead to deeper understanding, trust, and harmony among the nations and religions of our rapidly shrinking world. As is evidenced throughout recorded history, most wars have been attributed to the mistrust, intolerance, and fear surrounding another's religion. As Dennis Merritt Jones observed,

"Religion, whose purpose originally was to bring people together, (Greek/Latin word *religare* meaning 'to bind together) in many cases has done quite the opposite, dividing the world and separating its people, both from one another and from God. More wars have been fought in the name of God than for any other reason, as one religion deemed itself the one 'right one."

Increasingly, as social media unite the world's population, whether across town or across the planet, we are given a window into another's life, and often invited into their very soul, celebrating with them their joys, and mourning with them their losses. Once such a bond is formed, there is never again such a tendency toward mistrust and fear. We become better equipped to look past superficial differences, whether defined by ethnicity, race, or religion. We find another human being with similar values, hopes, and dreams.

As the world view testifies, and Facebook pages reflect, there are many paths to God or that Higher Power. Honor and respect must be given to each person's choice. Consider the illustration of a wagon wheel showing how the various different world religions relate to God. Imagine the outer rim of the wheel as humanity with God as the center hub, and all of the religions of the world being spokes running from the outer rim to the center. While the spokes all support the outer rim, they likewise all connect to God at the center.

Metaphysics and a Spiritual Approach to God

Certainly on the surface there seem to be vast differences among the world faiths. There is, however, more than just Facebook and social media uniting them. There is a "golden thread" running through all the great world religions. Looking at the commonality of these central principles can provide further understanding and answers toward ending the separation and fear humanity has long yearned to heal. Consider the possibility that all major world religions came into existence as a direct result of their founders reaching deep within their own spiritual nature and there touching the very face of God. Each religious leader, prophet, or holy man then deciphered these great truths and presented them in a way beneficial for the common man of their era and region. The study of these universal principles or central threads is often referred to as metaphysics.

Metaphysics is the branch of philosophy that examines the nature of reality, particularly the relationship between mind and matter. It is a study of the nonphysical laws or principles that govern the universe. "Meta" means above or beyond, and "physical" means material or that which is experienced by the five senses. It is the study of God as universal life principle, all-knowing, all-powerful, in and throughout all creation—everything we see, touch, smell, hear, taste, and beyond. Metaphysics is analogous to a generic approach to God. It is pure spirituality without the trappings, dogma, and doctrines, which are often more about the revealer of truth, and the many institutions formed thereafter than the truth that holy one shared. It is the study of the energies and forces innate to life, the common threads and principles interwoven into the parables and teachings of the world's great religions.

As an example of the universal nature of these truth principles, consider the Golden Rule. Below you will find how it appears in ten of the world's great religions:

The Golden Rule

Buddhism
Treat not others in ways that you yourself would find hurtful.
—The Buddha, Udana-Varga 5.1

Christianity
In everything, do to others as you would have them do to you;
for this is the law and the prophets.
—Jesus, Matthew 7:12

Confucianism
One word which sums up the basis of all good conduct....loving-kindness.
Do not do to others what you do not want done to yourself.
—Confucius, Analects 15.23

Hinduism

*This is the sum of duty: do not do to others
what would cause pain if done to you.*
—Mahabharata 5:1517

Islam

*Not one of you truly believes until you
wish for others what you wish for yourself.*
—The Prophet Muhammad, 13th of the 40 Hadiths of Nawawi

Jainism

One should treat all creatures in the world as one would like to be treated.
—Mahavira, Sutrakritanga

Judaism

*What is hateful to you, do not do to your neighbor.
This is the whole Torah; all the rest is commentary. Go and learn it.*
—Hillel, Talmud, Shabbath 31a

Sikhism

*I am a stranger to no one; and no one is a stranger to me.
Indeed, I am a friend to all.*
—Guru Granth Sahib, pg. 1299

Taoism

*Regard your neighbor's gain as your own gain
and your neighbor's loss as your own loss.*
—Lao Tzu, T'ai Shang Kan Ying P'ien, 213-218

Zoroastrianism

Do not do unto others whatever is injurious to yourself.
—Shayast-na-Shayast 13.29

As we further reflect on the relevance of these shared principles, let us consider that each of us also shares a portal to that same truth, that same wisdom, that same God or Higher Power. Spirituality is defined as direct knowing of God at our center, and while it is certain that our religious founders delved deep within its core waters, it is also within the capacity of each and every one of us to do the same. Spirituality is the understanding that we live in a spiritual universe with God at its center, as well as circumference. In other words God is all that is; and this God is all-loving, all-giving, and the very definition of good. It is my belief that as metaphysical principles and a spiritual approach to God become better known, understood, and applied, people will come to see truth as not just something contained in any certain religion, but as universal: That truth is the very nature of God and is in and throughout all life. And that, of course, includes each of us. There is no more direct approach to God than that found at the heart and center of our own being. Spirituality, then, is practicing the awareness of God's presence within us, and within everyone, and everything.

In conclusion, I share one of my great expectations for humanity, that as we continue to grow closer through Facebook and the many social networking technologies, we also begin to look beyond the ideologies and boundaries of religious and political traditions that have held us apart, and instead soften our gaze to view the other with more compassion and understanding, honoring the sacred presence of God within them, as well. I genuinely believe that as this unfolds the harsh and sometimes violent clashes among the world's great religions will be diminished. What greater gift could Mark Zuckerberg and Facebook promote in our world?

 Rev. Sandy H. M. Schwartz is a spiritual teacher, professional speaker, writer, certified LifeMastery consultant, coach, and ordained minister. Her vision and passion are assisting others to live the life of their greatest dreams. Our goals and dreams define who we are and who we are to become; and if there is a part of you aching to be more fully expressed, she would love to provide tools and direction for that to happen!

As an ordained New Thought minister, and director of a spiritual center, she has committed her life's work to the understanding, practice, and teaching of the laws that govern the universe. Therefore, she is uniquely qualified to be your guide on this journey. With over thirty years' experience implementing and teaching life success principles, she would love to share these principles with you now, providing inspiration, tools, and support for you to live the life of your greatest dreams!

https://www.facebook.com/RevSandySchwartz

Contact Info:
Facebook: Sandy H. M. Schwartz

Email:
Sandy@SandySchwartz.net
RevSandyS@aol.com

Web Site:
www.SandySchwartz.net

Chapter 14

Meet Jennifer Brocato of *Little Red Bird*

LIFE HASN'T ALWAYS BEEN easy for me. It certainly has given me its fair share of pain and demons to battle. Even so, I was never one to dwell on my struggles or project them to the world in a negative way. I have always continued to move forward, trying not to get in my own way. However, the grips of addiction sent me into a dark place for a very long time. It was a tough battle that taught me a lot about myself, as well as how I process the things that happen to me. There were times when I couldn't take the pain anymore. I can truly say that I am blessed to be here today.

As I journeyed along the road to sobriety and began to live a healthy life, I was not yet fully aware of all the signs, coincidences, and guidance already present in my life. I had always strongly believed that everything happens for a reason, but I didn't really understand the magnitude and divinity of my own perception.

Sadly, my younger sister, Mary, fell into the fatal hold of addiction. It was beyond painful for me to watch her hurt so deeply and have to go through things most of us only have nightmares about or see in movies.

She was a bright soul filled with love and an infectious spirit. Mary was a truly unique person—a real cheerleader in life who uplifted everyone with whom she came in contact. My little sis was the kind of person who didn't have to get to know you to decide if she liked you. She loved first. That was just who she was.

Her battle came to an end on March 22, 2008. She took her life in a moment of emotional duress, a spontaneous reaction with the utmost of consequences. Her loving heart was too broken and she could no longer bare the pain. Her light that had shinned so bright would be gone, and for her loved ones, this place would never be the same.

After receiving the news of her passing I was in total disbelief that she was gone. I couldn't fathom that I would never have the opportunity to hug her again or speak with her one last time. On the very day of receiving the news, while I was making arrangements to leave New York and fly home to Texas, filled with grief and pain, a little red cardinal landed on a shrub right in front of me. He startled me, so much so that I had to catch my breath. For a moment, I sat and looked at him in awe, numb. I was simply observing without thought, without pain. I was empty. I just sat there being, connected. I had lived in New York for many years, but I couldn't remember seeing a cardinal there, ever.

I flew to Texas the next day to prepare for Mary's funeral service. While driving to the funeral home, I looked outside my window to see none other than a cardinal flying right beside me. To my surprise, not one—but two—beautiful cardinals flew directly alongside my car for what seemed like an eternity. It was a surreal experience.

That's when my journey truly began.

Many circumstances surrounding Mary's passing could easily have consumed me, allowing my thoughts to dwell in perpetuity. However, this would have caused me more pain and suffering. Instead, I made the conscious decision to remember the good and the beauty that my sister brought to this world. I started a blog to honor her memory, and I began writing fairly regularly. It was an incredible source of healing for me. As I blogged about Mary and all the wonderful memories we shared, amazing things began to happen.

Signs and synchronicities were everywhere, and as my faith and acknowledgment of them grew, they increased tremendously. At moments, it was hard to believe that these things were actually happening. As I accepted the moments, my heart was filled with peace and joy. Many times I found myself asking my angels for a sign, and soon afterwards, I would see a cardinal in the most unlikely of places and times.

As I accepted these signs as Divine, more and more confirmations fell into place, at the most perfect times in my life. One after the other, incredible events transpired around me. My soul was open and ready to receive.

My feeling of grief and loss began to lessen as hope and love filled my heart more and more each day. Mary's passing was a heart-wrenching event, but from it sprung many wonderful things. While I miss her physical presence and the energy that she radiated, I have accepted it, as well as the pain that I felt. By allowing myself to experience my emotions and keeping my heart and soul open to her miraculous signs from above, the experience has changed me in the most profound ways. It has given me the opportunity to grow in ways I never thought possible.

Suffering opened my soul, because I let it be and accepted. My pain was so intense that I had to let it go. By letting it go, it freed me of attachments and resentments that held me captive. Suffering became my teacher, and ultimately, a source of gratitude. I am now able to experience pure beauty, love and joy. The signs and synchronicities have helped to heal me and answer some of my life's most difficult questions.

Choosing to let go, open up, and let love in has allowed me to recognize that our loved ones are never really gone. I came to understand the Divine presence and influences that are around us, all the time.

I felt lucky and blessed having these experiences, especially knowing how much suffering there is in life. I have learned that a negative can turn into positive, and light can shine on even the darkest parts of our souls if one is willing to be open, to love, and accept what is, knowing that it can all change.

I wanted to help those who were hurting and offer them inspiration through my own experience. The cardinal bird was so healing for me that, by allowing my sister's story to live on through me, I have been able to touch the lives of others who also are suffering.

Little Red Bird Chirps on Facebook was born June 5, 2011.

Little Red Bird Chirp's purpose is to reach anyone and everyone in need of some inspiration through love, faith, and hope by offering loving images, inspiring quotes and affirmations. I want to let people know that it's going to be okay and that life's greatest pains can be a catalyst to enlightenment. My personal experience of pain and suffering gave way to a new hope, strength, and understanding of life. I have learned that you have to give it away if you want to keep it; so helping others is an important part of my journey and purpose. As Little Red Bird Chirps has grown in community, so has my new awareness and presence of just "being." My hope and goal is that I am helping others to begin their own healing journey.

My mission with Little Red Bird Chirps is to inspire others to know and understand that we all have the power to heal and bring about immense positive change on our lives. It is my intention to continue to evolve spiritually by helping others to heal and find their true essence. I believe the true meaning of life is to develop our soul and help others discover theirs.

I have learned how to realize a deep and everlasting change by creating an internal shift brought on by an awareness and awaking consciousness. All of our struggles are lessons guiding us and teaching us what we are here to learn. By looking in the darkest areas of each of us, we allow the light in and break free from fear and worry, opening our hearts to give and receive love.

What was our worst pain and anguish can become a source of gratitude in its own way, by being our own greatest teacher and the catalyst to shedding ego and removing resistance and false attachments. In that process, one becomes awakened and aware of their true essence and purpose.

My loss and pain took a piece of my heart, but it also opened my soul in such a way that I will never be the same. Little Red Bird Chirps is here to heal those wishing to be healed, and it embodies my Mary's radiant and beautiful soul. She lives on through me to inspire, show love, open one's faith, and allow for hope.

 Jennifer Brocato is a spiritual warrior and an advocate for love, faith and hope. She lives her life trying to serve and help others, always looking for the next right thing to do. Her many trials and tribulations have truly been a defining source for her in bringing forth her true essence and purpose. She lives her life to be a power of example and a positive model for those seeking hope. She has created a Facebook community, Little Red Bird Chirps, to share some of her wisdom and insights.

https://www.facebook.com/littleredbirdchirps
http:// www.LovingMaryForever.com

Quotes from *Little Bird Chirps*

"It is in my darkest hour when I have learned my greatest lessons.
My pain was so great it defeated my own will, allowing
me to listen to the answers within."

"I'm not grateful for my losses—I'm grateful
for what my losses have taught me."

"When you focus on what really matters and you appreciate all that you
have in your life, all of a sudden the world isn't such a bad place after all!"

"Living in the presence with pure gratitude flowing from the
heart allows us to live with pure love passionately!"

"My decisions today will be for this day only. I can change
my mind tomorrow. Now is the only thing the matters."

"With my faith I am able to understand and know that I am right where I am
supposed to be. I may not have all that I want, but I have more than I need."

Chapter 15

Meet Vivek Subramaniam of the Idealist

As a child, I always felt that life was completely pointless. I hated every aspect of society—the way people treated their fellow human beings, the less privileged, other living things, and their own home planet. As I drifted further away from society, I began to understand why people are like this. I started to read more and to travel to different places around my country where there exists very high inequality. People are either very rich or very poor. There is no in-between. During my journey across India, I saw many things, including a man who was forced to eat his own human waste due to hunger and people who wasted millions in pubs and clubs. This was the first time I considered trying to make a change. It was at this time that I started my Facebook page, called the Idealist.

To be honest, my intention when I started this page was to talk mostly about political issues and to spread socialist and liberal-based economic ideas to as many people as I could. I was desperate to effect a change. As I began to understand the problem better, I realized that it was not political or economic but social. The mindset of people was what needed to change. All of this made me question what I wanted out of life. I realized that whatever I wanted, I needed to get it myself because no one was going to be around to do it for me. "The best day of your life is the one on which you decide your life is your own." I started to post content intended to make people more self-aware and more skeptical about the things they see and the things they teach their children, and to stop being slaves to the system.

Around this time, I came across a video by Jacque Fresco, which influenced me more than anything. He said, "The more justice you seek, the more hurt you become because there is no such thing as justice. There is whatever is out there. That's it." In other words, if people are conditioned to be racist bigots, if they are brought up in an environment that advocates that, how can you blame them for it? They are victims of a subculture. Therefore, they have to be helped.

The point is that we have to redesign the environment that produces aberrant behavior. That is the problem. The solution is not putting people in jail. Judges, lawyers, "freedom of choice" – such concepts are dangerous because they offer misinformation. They declare that the person is "bad" or that a person is a "serial killer." Serial killers are made, just as soldiers become serial killers with a machine gun. Soldiers become killing machines, but no one looks at them as murderers or assassins because that is "natural." So we blame people. We say, "Well, this guy was a Nazi; he tortured Jews." No, he was brought up to torture Jews.

"Once you accept the fact that people have individual choices, and they are free to make those choices..." Free to make choices means living without being influenced, and I cannot understand that at all. All of us are influenced in all of our choices by the culture we live in, by our parents, and by the values that dominate. Since we are influenced, there cannot be "free" choices. For example, if you were to ask someone, what is the greatest country in the world? The true answer would be: "I have not been all over the world, and I do not know enough about different cultures to answer that question." I do not know anyone who speaks that way. They say, "It's the good ole U.S.A.! The greatest country in the world!" There is no probing, "Have you been to India?" "No." "Have you been to England?" "No." "Have you been to France?" "No." "Then what do you base your assumptions on?" They cannot answer. They get mad at you. They say, "God dammit?! Who the hell are you to tell me what to think?!" Remember, you are dealing with aberrant people. They are not responsible for their answers. They are victims of culture, and that means they have been influenced by their culture.

Eventually, I started to share posts on my page that encouraged people to find what they wanted within themselves and to find things that agreed with their own reasoning. I started to understand and see everything more clearly. I understood that most of the things that people say and think result from the childhood indoctrination that they received. This is when I started to take Buddhism very seriously. I read many scriptures and even met a number of Buddhist monks. I stopped watching TV completely. As I understood more, I came to realize that I know nothing, and before I start to change others, I should start with myself. I became more socially active, friendlier, and kinder to others.

Now it has been over a year since I started this page and I can say without a doubt that this page has given more to me than I have given to it. I have started to be more open to new ideas, and, most importantly, I have found people who see the way I see life. I have realized how great life is. As Gandhi said once, "Humanity is an ocean; if a few drops of the ocean are dirty, the ocean does not become dirty."

Vivek Subramaniam is a graduate student. Born and raised in India, he is an active member of Students Federation of India.

http://www.facebook.com/TheIDEAlistRevolution
http://www.theidealistrevolution.com/

Chapter 16

Meet Sue Krebs of Soul Speaking

My whole life has been quietly directing me to this magnificent now moment. While it's hardly been a straight path, I can certainly appreciate how every experience, the good and the bad, has contributed to bringing me here—poised to fly to heights scarcely imagined just a short time ago.

I experienced very early on the joy and satisfaction of excelling at whatever I focused on. I loved to learn and pushed myself beyond normal expectations. More was always better. By the eighth grade, I was attending the local high school for geometry classes. By the time I graduated from high school, I had two years of college calculus credits to my name. It seemed to make sense to turn my apparent aptitude for math and science into an engineering degree and eventually a professional structural engineering license. Eventually I learned that simply doing what you are good at because someone else said you should does not necessarily lead to happiness. I left a job as head structural engineer at a design architectural and engineering firm to go back to school to get a master's degree in Adlerian counseling and psychotherapy, this time following my heart.

Looking back now, I can see that this was a pivotal point in my life. Within a year, I entered therapy to address my childhood sexual abuse by my brother, met the man who would become my husband, toured Europe with other 20-somethings, quit my engineering job, and started grad school. As I've come to recognize about myself, I dive into things wholeheartedly. I was ready to remake my life, and I undertook the overhaul with gusto.

Intertwined through this entire journey was my desire to understand life spiritually. Raised in a strict Catholic family and educated in a parochial grade school, my spiritual roots were firmly entrenched in the dogma of a church filled with inconsistencies and contradictions, motivated by fear and governed by guilt. Intuitively I knew that there was more to God than this, and for years, I sought to discover for myself what the "more" might be. My searching took me both closer to and then eventually far away from the Catholic traditions. Superimposed on my life was a fascination and a connection to the paranormal and the psychic. It was not until just a few years ago that my interest and desire to be psychic (whatever that actually meant) collided head-on with my intense longing to understand life spiritually.

Just five years ago, I found myself married and a stay-at-home mother of three young boys. I also now owned a home-based scrapbooking business. I traveled across the country selling my own album kits and other scrapbook supplies at scrapbook conventions and expos. I taught classes promoting my kits and gaining valuable experience in connecting with audiences both large and small. After a number of years of designing and manufacturing my own kits, I knew my heart really was not in this anymore. I loved the traveling, and I loved connecting with people. I just did not love the production side of my business.

About this time, on a flight to a scrapbook show in Salt Lake City, I read *The Secret,* and something significant shifted within me. I began seeking more information about this human potential movement, the law of attraction and how we are each responsible for creating our own reality. Then another significant occurrence took place. A friend from Salt Lake City whom I was just getting to know invited me to join her in having my first psychic reading. Without knowing it, my fascination with the paranormal was now on a collision course with my spirituality.

My interest in authors and teachers, psychics, and energy healers blossomed. I read works by Sylvia Browne, Neale Donald Walsch, James Redfield, Wayne Dyer, Eckhart Tolle, and Sonia Choquette, to name just a few. The more I read, the greater my thirst for understanding grew. I began finding teachers online, participating in teleclasses and teleseminars. Then in October 2009, I attended a four-day Six-Sensory Certification Training by Sonia Choquette in Chicago, and my whole world transformed. I finally understood that I am so much more than this physical expression of me. I am a divine, spiritual, eternal being of light, and I am intimately connected to all that is.

This training program fed my soul in ways I'd never experienced. It opened doors to arenas that I didn't even know existed, and opportunities to learn and experience more flooded in. When I encountered the healing energies of Reiki a few months later, I knew that I had to learn Reiki for myself and quickly attained master level in the Usui Reiki tradition. The same thing happened when I stumbled across information about the Akashic records online. I began studying and accessing the records myself, finally training with Linda Howe, head and founder of the Linda Howe Center for Akashic Studies. I began to embrace the energetic nature of life and strived to develop my sensitivity to the subtle nuances surrounding us. My passion for living life in this way continued to grow as I experienced the power of implementing these concepts.

In the course of my explorations, I met many wonderful people who have contributed to my understanding and practice of life as the flow of energy. I attracted the teachings of Abraham-Hicks which felt like the energetic equivalent of "coming home." Together, these new friends and I have learned, practiced, played, expanded, and embraced this energetic explanation of the way life works. And it was at this point in my journey that Facebook came to play an instrumental role as well.

One day, I found that my scrapbooking website had been deleted by the hosting company because hackers had compromised it and were now using it for their own nefarious agendas. I took this to be a "push" from the universe to pursue my dream of connecting with people at a soul level, of encouraging them to acknowledge their power to create their lives and to empower them to live joyously. Facebook provided me with the opportunity and the means to find the very people ready to hear my message.

It took several months of playing on Facebook to learn my way around, to discover groups, and eventually to learn how to build my fan page Soul Speaking. Gradually the number of followers on my page grew, slowly at first and then with a steady consistency. Approximately one year after I really began building my page, Soul Speaking now has 50,000 followers, a fact that continues to astound me!

I am still on my own journey, striving to live in truth and alignment with my highest self. Providing Akashic Record Readings and Cultivating Joy Sessions (my unique form of life coaching) through my Facebook connections allows me the great joy of connecting at the soul level with amazing people all across the world. My life has become one of infinite possibilities, and sharing this perspective with others just increases the joy in my own life. Whatever we focus on grows! I've deliberately chosen to focus on the wonder and magic that life holds. And in response, my life has become truly wondrous and magical.

 Sue Krebs has worn many hats as she has journeyed through this life: mom to three inspiring boys, wife of eighteen years to her wonderful husband, former structural engineer, therapist, entrepreneur, and many, many more. While these describe some aspects of who she is, she also recognizes that she is so much more. She is a lover of life, a student, a seeker, a teacher, a writer, and a healer. More than all of these, she is a spiritual being having a most magnificent physical experience. She offers her unique and uplifting perspective to clients around the world through Akashic Record Readings and her unique form of life coaching called Cultivating Joy Sessions.

www.facebook.com/SoulSpeaking
www.suekrebs.wordpress.com

Chapter 17

Meet Gabriella Boaehmer and Jim Camut of *HeartMath*

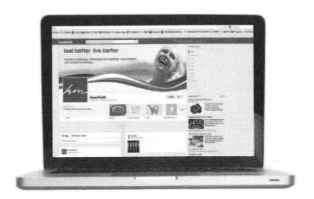

Keeping the Heart on Facebook

Wherever there are people there are surely hearts, and as Facebook grows—connecting people, preferences, stories, pictures and emoticons—there is also a vast network of hearts that are also connecting through the inspirational work of an organization called HeartMath.

HeartMath has harnessed the power of social media to connect countless people with like-hearted interest. Fans gain daily inspiration from the folks at HeartMath whose mission is all about improving people's lives through research-based tools and techniques that reduce stress, increase personal resilience, and improve the emotional aspects of life.

On the HeartMath Facebook page we're helping people reflect on living more from the heart, or what we call heart-based living. This is where we qualify our perceptions and interactions with life and others through the heart, which creates personal alignment with our authentic nature and our core heart values. We want the page to remind people that life is good, people are good, and that when we chose to live life more from the heart we can make a difference in our own lives and in the lives of those we care about. Ultimately, we can make a difference by adding more goodness and heart to the world around us.

HeartMath's friends are dedicated and they're touched by the kind of outreach they experience from HeartMath, leaving comments on our page such as these:

I hardly have words sufficient to express how very GRATEFUL I am for the brilliant and effective work that HeartMath does. THANK YOU.

I just finished reading *The Hidden Power of the Heart* for perhaps the 6th time (since it was first published in 1991) The brilliance HeartMath program is profound - and so very needed at this time.

The Practicality of *HeartMath*

What is truly unique about HeartMath is how it has added science and research to what might otherwise seem to some people like philosophical fluff. More than two decades ago, way before Facebook was even a glimmer in Mark Zuckerberg's eye, the HeartMath research team began uncovering new understandings about stress and emotions. HeartMath researchers conducted studies, which went on to be published in numerous peer-review journals, demonstrating a critical link among emotions, heart function, and cognitive performance.

One of key discoveries made by HeartMath is that different emotions create different rhythmic patterns within the heart. We found that when people learn to change the rhythms of their heart, they can reduce the amount of stress they experience. These understandings about the heart are brought to the HeartMath Facebook page every day.

Underneath all the button clicking and posting is a team of people that truly care about others. Our mission is about inspiring people to enrich their lives, and to help them honor and connect with their deeper more authentic selves. HeartMath is known not only for its science and research, but also for the system that has evolved from it. The HeartMath system consists of tools, techniques, programs, and technologies designed to provide stepping stones for helping people connect with the intelligence and guidance of their own hearts.

Our outreach for HeartMath through our Facebook page is an all-inclusive experience: We embrace people from all walks of life, all cultures, all ages, and all backgrounds. The HeartMath system provides universal methods that help people improve the quality of their life experience every day.

Loyal fans stop by our Facebook page habitually—like going to a favorite coffee house to grab a little java for a pick-me-up—except on our page we're serving up inspiration. We like to help people find a fresh perspective, a ray of hope or a reminder that friends, family, and core heart values—such as gratitude, care, compassion and love—are what really matter. Often, remembering the things that do matter and really feeling them is enough to help offset whatever little irks, irritations, or frustrations might have popped up that day. And when circumstances are tougher and stress has a tighter grip, the HeartMath System provides solutions to help people regain the inner balance they crave, so they can start releasing stress and find new ways to deal with challenges as they arise.

The menu of inspiration on our Facebook page includes daily heart quotes, heart intelligence tips, and exercises designed to refresh the mind, body, heart, and soul. Our fans appreciate the variety and our posts evoke comments such as these:

I did this [exercise] last night prior to getting to sleep and I was out in no time with the most restful sleep. Every day as I focus on the heart energy of Love and gratitude my life improves tremendously.

Great exercise worth practicing!

Yes I'll try this, thanks again...!!!

Thanks I needed that heart + math ≈ peace...!!

Thank you for offering such useful information that we can all put to use.

Connected in Heart

As a very prominent component to our page, we want HeartMath to exemplify the bond of human connection. The notion that we're all connected to one another has been written about for centuries. We've all witnessed this human connection at its best when natural disasters or major crises hit: People come together helping one another for the good of humanity.

In crises people's hearts come alive and they freely offer their compassion, love, generosity, and care. This heart component of humanity is powerful and dynamic. It feels right, natural, and deep when we engage it. HeartMath is helping to make a difference by inspiring people to connect with these innate heart qualities, without the circumstances of crisis or catastrophe. The world needs this level of care and connection every day, not just when people are suffering.

As HeartMath research shows, something amazing happens when you focus on your heart and intentionally generate a positive feeling— whether love for a pet, a sentiment of gratitude to a dear friend, or any heartfelt positive emotion. When a positive emotion is embraced, the heart's rhythms begin to change into a more ordered pattern. The rhythms look smooth and ordered when plotted on a graph, like rolling hills and valleys. As these rhythms take form something even more amazing happens: Brainwave patterns begin to synchronize with the heart. This synchronization impacts the entire body. In other words, the ordered rhythms of the heart entrain the entire body to a harmonious and balanced state.

In this state, which science calls "coherence," there is an increased heart flow about life. While in coherence we experience improved cognitive functioning; the hormonal system becomes more balanced; our immune system gets a boost; DHEA, the antiaging hormone, increases while cortisol, often called the stress hormone, decreases; and measurable intuitive abilities also increase. This is a positive feeling state with physical, emotional, mental, and some might even say spiritual benefits. It is the ideal state of human functioning that's coded in our DNA.

As much as these positive emotions feel great, we also know it's only human to experience stress, which we all have to varying degrees. You've probably seen friends venting political, social, and personal life frustrations on Facebook; it's commonplace.

Contrary to the ordered state of heart coherence, stress—or incoherence—is another state that many are all too familiar with. While experiencing stress, the heart's rhythms become chaotic and the coherent heart-brain synchronization diminishes. The heart emits erratic rhythms that look much like an earthquake on a seismograph, as a jagged and irregular pattern. This stress reaction ripples throughout the body almost instantaneously and triggers our more primitive fight-or-flight reactions to ordinary life situations.

While stress can't always be avoided, we can learn to change our response to it. HeartMath is showing people how they can use their hearts to find their way back to an inner balance, or coherent state, where we're connected with our authentic selves and have a deeper connection with others. This is the place where life feels better.

HeartMath has a tagline that says, "A Change of Heart Changes Everything," and it's true! As we learn to change the rhythms of the heart, we start to feel different, we see things differently, and we become more of who we truly are. The heart has a way of bringing out the best of people and perhaps why so many people like coming to the HeartMath Facebook page.

Gabriella Boehmer
Director of Public Relations
Gabriella has always possessed a passion for personal growth and a desire to help others. Realizing her dream to cultivate both of these areas, she signed on with HeartMath more than twenty years ago as the director of public relations. Gabriella directs all media relation activities, including all the social media platform activities for HeartMath. She brings an undeniable tenacity and fresh creativity to the orchestration of all the company's media campaigns.

Gabriella says that working with HeartMath is more than a job; it has enriched the fabric of her life beyond measure, both personally and professionally.

Jim Camut
Public Relations Assistant, Social Media Specialist
Jim's inclination has always been to pour his heart into anything he does and follow his heart's compass in all endeavors. It's led him around the world as a competitive cyclist racing in amateur to professional ranks, but Jim hung up his racing wheels several years ago to join HeartMath, having taken a cue from his heart to do so.

Keeping his full-speed-ahead racing charisma, Jim helps to sustain HeartMath's media and social media outreach, while also developing copy, graphics, and web pages to educate others in the practicality of heart intelligence.

https://www.facebook.com/HeartMath

Chapter 18

Meet Zdravko Stefanovic of *Share Your Care*

I WAS QUITE A TROUBLED SOUL not so long ago. Having the privileges of a good job with a good salary, a nice apartment, a nice way of earning money and saving up for future investments, I was still troubled. I knew not why I was troubled, but deep inside I felt that whatever I was doing within the domain of this acquired economic safety, I was still missing parts that were turning my materialistic values into mere misery.

It was not until one event where my entire world of existence was smashed into pieces that out came clarity, love, peacefulness, wisdom, discipline, tolerance, generosity, gratefulness, and compassion.

The experience of pure consciousness was the rock that smashed the glasshouse that I was living in. Coming in touch with the source, the source within me, was the door that I had yet not walked through although it felt as if it was my point of existential origin. We all have this door within ourselves that leads to beautiful insights. Insights such as: The materialistic values that we have been taught to appreciate and strive for our entire lives are a lie; to appreciate what we have and not becoming depressed over what we don't have; to learn that we are all truly equal in our constructional parameters, that we are organisms of beautiful potential but most of us have been thrown into a world where linear values only lead to disappointment. A bigger house, a better car, better clothes—we have become obsessed with valuing the things that have the least value.

This was the lie or illusion that I was living in. This is the lie and illusion that most of my fellow brothers and sisters live in. We are constantly in search of more and more, instead of pausing for a second to look around us. Look within ourselves and become truly aware of ourselves and the clockwork that is taking place inside ourselves.

During the experience of pure consciousness, I had heard the word "Buddha" repeated a couple of times. I remembered it, since it was not something I was familiar with at that time. After that experience, I looked it up and besides the fact that it often refers to Siddhartha Gautama, the founding father of Buddhism, its definition within Buddhism means the "enlightened one" or the "awakened one." It surely matched the current state of mind that I was in. In this state where my mind was as open as the sun that illuminates a dark room, I glanced at the objects that were surrounding me. It was clear to me that these objects had absolutely no significance to my own existence as an organism of dreams, hopes, orgasms, chemistry, physics, and so on; they were simply not relevant. And they still aren't.

I have come to understand that humans have very few basic needs but endless wants. To live, appreciate, and pay attention to every moment of my own existence has become my pleasure. Attention costs no money, my only investment is training. Through the method of meditation, I have the ability to go deep within myself and find the inner peace that I once lacked. The secret of happiness, you see, is not found in seeking more, but in developing the capacity to enjoy having less.

Most of us in the Western technocratic world aren't used to this concept. We use, grab, trash, sometimes recycle, and consume as much as we possibly can. This leads mankind into a terrible trap that will back-fire on each individual and create a loop of misery and the devastation of this beautiful planet. Instead of planning your next vacation, perhaps you need to create a life that you don't want to flee from.

So I started reading a lot. I considered everything that came my way to be a source of possible inspiration or knowledge. I woke up with a smile on my face every day. Not because I had received my salary or had a fresh new pair of jeans, but because I was *alive*. I was breathing. Every heartbeat was the continuous and ongoing proof that I had the ability to alter the state of mind that I was living in. The cosmic surroundings around me and everything within them were beautiful. They made up the current field of perception that I was gazing on and paying attention to; every detail was becoming a neurological and existential pleasure of mine. I started to think that everything around me is a product of the universe itself, including me, and so it is. We are the universe, express-ing ourselves as humans for a little while. I began to love everything and everyone for no apparent reason except one: because I *can*.

Everything that makes up the universe, including me, you, and everything that you know to exist vibrates. Vibration is the consequence of energy. When you analyze any object or living creature, it consists of molecular and atomic structures. Carbon, oxygen, nitrogen, protons, neutrons, electrons, quarks. When you go and dig a little deeper on a microscopic, subatomic, and subnuclear level, you will find out that par-ticles are replaced with the concept of waves, which are made up of the same things thoughts are made of.

Depending on whether your thoughts are driven by love or fear, you will affect yourself and your surroundings accordingly. All our feel-ings can be put into two categories: love or fear. The frequency of love is much more intense than fear. It goes up and down rapidly while the frequency of fear is slow and not as close and intense as love. All feelings can be linked to either one of them. That is why love, when applied in the most altruistic way possible, makes you happy, happy for no reason. When you do something for someone not expecting anything in return, you are demonstrating how beautiful your actions can be and you are successfully affecting your own existence and the existence of others.

When I came to the realization that "what we think, we become," my life changed dramatically. I understood that we really have the ability to shape our own realities and how we decide to live each day of our lives. How we are all one. Instead of thinking in terms of separation, I began to reason in terms of unity. How we actually are the same. Society doesn't provide much support for this. We are constantly bombarded by information that separates us, instead of connecting us. Sexuality, social status, income, materialistic possessions, skin color; the list goes on. They have no meaning whatsoever in terms of each and every one of the subjective experiences of consciousness that we all have. That is to say, *your life.*

The biggest change I started to apply in my life was to really get to know myself, *without the impact of others.* By actually listening to my thoughts and asking myself whether each thought had a positive or a negative impact on my life, I started living much easier. I categorized what I actually *needed* and what I *wanted.* For example: Do I really need a pair of new shoes? Do I really need to have a car?

I started to live more simply. After the experience of pure consciousness, I had lost my source of income. Luckily, I had gotten to the realization that I really don't need that many things in life in order to live. I lived with my mom and we had it rough. We ate whatever there was to eat and on the love that we shared with each other. I told my mom that I was glad that I was alive and that I was with her and that I really didn't need much more than that. Since I am human like the rest of us, our needs are universal.

I quit having a vague image of my everyday life. I had a complete, aware, and blissful everyday experience through the simple way of living and appreciating what I had, not craving for more. Meditation was a good step for me. Buddhism gave me clarity and wisdom in life. Books gave me knowledge. By listening to my inner self, I started to feel real, altruistic love toward everything. I began to exercise a lot and through the words of Buddha I understood that "To keep the body in good health is a duty...otherwise we shall not be able to keep our mind strong and clear."

I stopped paying attention to the media, newspapers and TV. It was hard in the beginning, but later on I noticed how much less I was being obsessed with information that has literally *no* importance to my own living. I had one and one goal only: *to keep my mind clear. Our own biggest, personal enemy is our ego. Our ego is what stops us from truly showing ourselves through honesty, compassion, and love.*

What I noticed in my awakening is that people tend to relate their current state of existence to a previous occurrence. I try to tell people that the past is nonexistent. It exists purely in your mind. Make of it what you can, if you can, to benefit your current moment. The future is also nonexistent. It also exists only in your mind. What I'm trying to say with all this is that to understand the basic principles of living, you must first learn how to live. If you are living in the domains of the nonexistent then you are not living. Breathe the air you're in. Gaze on the stars you're beneath. Feel the ground with your bare feet. Love your spouse. Love your dog. Love any stranger who passes you by. Appreciate the existence of a tree that's maybe in front of you, that's constantly converting the air into oxygen, so that you can breathe and continue to live. When you have started to see things for what they really are and not caring if Paris Hilton has a new dog or if Johnny Depp is starring in the new Quentin Tarantino movie, you are actually living. Do not care for cultural values set by the majority of people. Create your own perception. Create your own values. Even if some of your friends, colleagues, or relatives at first may not see what you see, it is important to remember that your life is a subjective experience. Only you can see what you see from the point you're currently standing on. You will find out that everything that connects you with the universe and everything within you truly is love. We are beautiful creatures. We are caring creatures. We are loving creatures. We are almost magical, if you ask me. We must just remember that the mind is everything. What you think, you will become.

Bless

Zdravko Stefanovic

Twenty-three and living in Sweden, Zdravko administers the page *Share Your Care*, where he features inspirational quotes, proverbs, texts, and good deeds, all intended to inspire others to create a wave of good deeds that might spread across the globe. He believes this will happen when his group has grown a bit more. Zdravko is now on the path to becoming a professional diver and working around the world. He is deeply interested in philosophy, shamanism, healing, nature, yoga, quantum mechanics, and themes that inspire his consciousness to grow. Meditation and Buddhism inspire him and guide his evolving self-image. Zdravko also has a blog where he shares his own writing, some in Swedish and some in English.

https://www.facebook.com/share.your.care.today
http://www.facebook.com/ConsciousnessEvolution
http://www.consciousness-evolution.org/

Chapter 19

Meet Gigi Galluzzo of *Inspired Intentions*

PASSION WAS ALWAYS THE fashion within the four walls of the home in which I was raised. I was born into a wonderfully spirited Italian/ Irish Catholic family. There was never a dull moment! I was the fifth child of six delightful beings born to George and Jackie Bocci. As a youth, much of my time was spent observing others, as I was blessed with asthma, and I do mean blessed! Through the ongoing adversity of my disease, I learned so much! The challenges of life bring about the most noteworthy growth.

The glass has always been more than half full for me, and my positive mental attitude allowed me to thrive. I grew to understand that there is always so much more than meets the eye. As a communications major in college, I discovered that words are such a gift, and the numerous modes by which we communicate with one another vary in power and intensity. I have taken part in many forms of media, and I have found Facebook to be the very best forum to reach people and from all over the world simultaneously—and instantly.

I am a writer, poet, and Life Coach who thrives on helping and consoling those who have difficulty in helping themselves. My business is called "Inspired Now." I have written for many years about the blessing that this life truly is. My personal intention has always been the same: to aspire to help others discover themselves through me. I started my personal Facebook page in the fall of 2009. I found it to be an extraordinary way to keep in touch with family and friends whom I didn't see often. As my Facebook page grew, so did I.

In 2010, I made the decision to leave my husband of 26 years. Throughout the early days of my legal separation, my writing increased daily. The trials within my life left me with plenty to write about. The more difficult my life became, the more clearly I was able to see. My mind was fertile with new ideas for a happier life, which I knew was just ahead. I began writing quotes and poems to inspire others at first, but I realized I was helping myself, as well.

The response to my quotes was favorable, as my fan base grew and expanded into other spaces. I saw my quotes being used by all kinds of community efforts, from childhood bullying outreach programs to "how to stay fit" newsletters, as well as other pages and blogs throughout the Internet. In the summer of 2010, I was approached to write for a Facebook community page, as an administrator. At the time, I didn't really understand what that meant. It wasn't long, however, before my wheels were turning quickly in a positive direction. So many people approached me to find out who I was and where I came from. It was an exciting time indeed. The world I had known was ending and a bright new future was being formed in front of my eyes.

I still write original pieces for that first Facebook page. In addition, I write for several other inspirational pages, including two of my own. My interests prompted me to become involved with dozens of community groups, where I interact with like-minded friends interested in everything from poetry to insightful meanderings.

My first inspirational community page, entitled "Inspired Intentions," took seed during the summer of 2011. On that page I post original quotes and poems embedded on images and pictures from around the world. People often send me pictures so I can personalize them with an inspirational quote written just for them, by me. People visit the page and are quickly inspired, and they often share my work on their own pages. Nothing delights me more than by inspiring others to want more for themselves. I am grateful beyond all my words to be able to touch others the way I do. I am personally inspired by each moment of my life. What a journey this experience is! I sustain my world by nourishing it with as many positive thoughts as possible. I became filled with dreams of what I knew would be my fabulous future. I was writing more and more every day. It was my dream to become published, so I could reach even more people, and do more to help others as they walk the path alongside me. To welcome people to my page, I offer new Facebook travelers this message: "Inspired Intentions is a place for you to rejuvenate and become uplifted as you go about the day."

It pleases me greatly to write quotes and poetry so others might see the light that they truly are. I share this with those who visit my page: "Life is about you, all the time...how you feel, what you think about, and what you dream about within each and every moment of every day. You are wise and wonderful all the time! See the doorways and not the doors as you make your way through the day. Come by Inspired Intentions for a fresh dose of support. New posts arrive on a continual basis, as I write constantly. I look forward to touching you in some way through your imagination, where all the greatness is manifested into life, one moment at a time. Feel free to think and wonder, wonder and create all that you so desire."

My First Book

One of the great people whom I have met through Facebook discovered me while I was writing on my first page. The topic of our conversations ran the gamut from life's complexities to staying within a constant positive flow. This all occurred while he was battling cancer. The result of our mutual inspiration and the power of a positive mindset were twofold: My friend checked his cancer at the door—and I learned a great deal from the teacher that he would always be to me.

In early spring of 2011, the same fellow writer and Facebook friend approached me about the effect my inspirational work and words were having on people. Because of what he witnessed, he extended an offer to assist me in getting my words in book form to more effectively spread inspiration and hope to the world. At that moment, the importance of self-produced inspirational quotations became my calling. I am happy to announce that my first book, *The Light House Call*, is in the final stages at Balboa publishing.

"Quotes are indeed a powerful means to inspire, educate and otherwise touch someone's heart, mind and soul. What a gift it is to give a thought, a prayer or an idea on the wings of a message. Like many other forms of artistic expression, the quote has the ability to touch others deeply and profoundly, so much so, that quotes become known and repeated by whole societies."
—Gigi Galluzzo

The Light House Call features quotes and poems written for or about so many people I have had the pleasure of meeting through Facebook. Most of the images used in the book are my own, but there are some from wonderful photographers that I have met by way of Facebook. During the fall of 2012, I began collaborating with my fiancé on a Facebook page entitled *Love Finally Found*. The pieces for this page are about love. As he and I bask in the wonderment and gift that love truly is, we share our insights on this fan page. That page was inspired by my evolution over the many months of writing on Facebook. You see, the love of life was ever present within me, but until the summer of 2012, I had no one with whom to share this greatness. Now, travelers to *Love Finally Found* will be greeted with these words:

"When we love and are loved in return, it is the closest thing to a real magic trick we all can perform. For it is indeed love that keeps this great place magnificent!

"Love is the reason for everything that we do, *always*! This new page was developed to show, by example, love to another, while sharing love with you all. Within this writer's page you will find quotes and images that will inspire. We invited you to please join us, and feel free to post your favorite sayings and images that show love and share love from your perspective."

As an "emotional sponge," I have found it vital to know how to avoid taking on negative emotions from other individuals. Through my Facebook pages, I am able to help others more effectively now, without getting too entangled regarding the issues they bring to me. I have learned to be more emotionally free, while helping others to do the same. The wondrous mechanism of Facebook has transformed my life from what was, to what is today.

I will continue to reinvent my "wheel" with ease, through this unique portal in cyberspace known as Facebook Inspirational Fan Pages. I look to draw out the positive in people in all situations, as I relish in seeing the good in others. I enjoy spending time with others who affirm the bright side of life. I delight in creating inspirational words and images. Inspiration is often contagious, and I intend to spread more than my share of it in this world.

We all strive for a victorious walk through this life, and I have experienced the most wondrous transformation on Facebook. The journey that I am on is one of daily accomplishments. My personal life has been enriched and my passion for life has been restored. I am encouraged that my future will bring even greater insight. I am so very fortunate to have been introduced to Facebook by my wonderful daughter. It has been a vessel where I give others inspiration and hope, as well as quench my thirst for helping others. I look forward to all of the greatness that I know Facebook will continue to be as I walk down the wondrous path within this magnificent life.

 Gigi Galluzzo has lived her entire life in the Pacific Northwest, until recently. She worked more than 30 years in the medical industry, and she worked in radio broadcasting. When Gigi started writing in 2010, it was to gather her own thoughts and recognize the blessings of her own life. Before long, people began to acknowledge the beautiful and inspiring words that seemed to flow from her pen. From her humble

beginnings until the start of this book, her followers have grown by the thousands and now include people from around the world who wake up every morning to her inspirational words and are strengthened by reading them. Her energy and endless sharing are certain to provide all of us with hope and strength to overcome any of life's adversities. We are all blessed, because God and the universe are working overtime through this wonderful lady.

https://www.facebook.com/pages/Inspired-Intentions
https://www.facebook.com/pages/Love-Finally-Found

Chapter 20

Meet Mauricio Ramos Fonseca of
The Global Informer

Behind Global Informer

GLOBAL INFORMER HAS as its purpose to post important information, in the form of pictures and videos, in several languages, for all people, concerning the following topics: human rights, child labor, crimes
against democracy, political corruption, extremism religion, international traffic, and crimes against animal life and nature. This has been
my page description since February 2011.

Global Informer did not start on Facebook. Years before, people used
to print fanzines to distribute for free at universities, colleges, and schools.
Most were particularly motivated by political issues. I was there printing
mine under the Portuguese name "O Informante." The topics I wrote about
included politics, art, and culture. I drew some illustrations and invited
other designers and graphic artists in the university also to contribute.

Why was I writing about politics? Was I trying to change the world? Let me share a little about my country's recent history.

In the mid sixties and seventies, Brazil was suffering a repression (military regime) and most of our rights of expression were abolished. The right of speech, free journalism, and art and cultural expressions were all repressed by the military government, as had happened all over Latin America. I was born in 1979, at the end of that regime (the military left power in 1984 when a new civilian president was elected indirectly by Parliament), so I did not have to fight against the oppressors like many others before me. My youth became characterized by a kind of frustration and apathy. Without real enemies, I could find no reason to mobilize.

In 1989 another civilian was elected president, this time by popular vote. Since then, all of the presidents, majors, and congressmen are chosen by vote. Social inequality decreased, but on the other hand corruption still continues. Our society, in particular the youth, seems to be anaesthetized. Society reflects a natural conformism as a result of social development. This attitude of immobility is harmful to the political system but allows corruption to flourish.

Indeed my generation lived the hangover after the big party that lasted from the sixties to the eighties. The upset decade coincided with a depressive time for me personally. I was part of the nineties youth without real enemies to fight against, living in loneliness every day. I suffered depression like many other teenagers. I remember spending entire afternoons alone listening to music, drawing, or reading. These solitary behaviors molded my personality.

I started attending the university at the age of 17 to study communication, even though I had not communicated with people very much in my life. I was introverted and had a tendency to think everyone around me was boring or stupid. I had also played the guitar for years, practicing every day. However, because of my introverted behavior, I gave up any aspirations for a career as a musician. First of all, I was never interested in performing for people in bars or pubs, and second, I felt sickened to think about rehearsing with other guys as a band.

It took some years for me to figure out that my personality was much more suited to be a writer, working on my own rather than in a group. Finally, I understood that the world needs all kind of people, the ones to work in groups or communities and the ones to be alone. Many great writers, painters, and composers, as well as many unknown artists, had to be alone to write, to feel the life around them, and to comprehend human nature.

This is not to say that I was seeking glory as a famous writer or philosopher. I wrote some short stories, a monologue, and screenplays. However, none of my writing has yet been published as a book because we are living in new times, shifting the paper to the digital. The public now seems less interested in literature; reading is no longer as fun as it used to be. Internet, social media, video games, and gadgets are winning the public's attention.

Because publishers are not supporting new authors and creating a book is so hard, I instead decided to work with audiovisual media (an idea in the head, a camera in the hand). For the past few years, I have been producing video arts, influenced by art movements and mixing techniques from many sources. My aim is not to have an audience or to be famous. This is just my way to spend my time and have fun.

I am a person interested in arts and culture. Since my childhood, I have spent and wasted my insomnia writing, reading, and watching movies, with many languages, messages, and faces. I believe artistic diversity has the power not to change the world but to make the individual more open-minded. That does not mean to be happier—happiness is an abstraction—but to give the power to everyone to question reality. Give freedom, more than any political party or system. It is based on this ideology that Global Informer was created.

For the future, I am beginning to create a mobile device application and a website to give to Global Informer users a smaller platform different from Facebook but providing a space to write about science, art, and free journalism. I envision it as a kind of blog service via social media interface for mobile devices. At the moment I just have the name and some experimental templates. In order to make this project real, I will need to find some people and work as a team, something for me which is not so cool, but that is the irony. Living and changing, or better, living and learning.

 Maurício Ramos Fonseca was born in São Paulo, the largest Brazilian city (about twelve million people), also largest in Latin America. After graduating in communication, arts and marketing, he started working with audiovisual artwork, producing video arts and performances between the years 2006 and 2009. He entered his video artwork in digital new media festivals.

He founded Global Informer blog and Facebook page in 2011. Before the Facebook platform, Global Informer was a fanzine (in Portuguese version) newspaper, created with collaborators and distributed for free in several universities. The publication contains writing about politics, society, art, and behavior. In February 2011, just as a pastime, it was launched in English and Spanish for spreading the latest news about the riots for freedom in the Middle East.

Nowadays, Global Informer reaches 60,000 fans and the contents have suffered some changes. It is now focused on political issues as well as the culture and history. Global Informer is part of a freedom information pages networks that every day shares pictures and links with almost one million users.

We are working on a new platform, an app to permit users to write, produce, and share contents, articles specifically on science and technology, through a mobile connection, without the current Facebook censorship.

http://www.flickr.com/photos/maulsoleu
(My illustrations and street arts)

www.facebook.com/globalinformer

http://www.YouTube.com/user/maulsoleu/
videos?flow=grid&view=0
(YouTube channel with some of my videos)

http://theglobalinformer.wordpress.com
http://www.facebook.com/mausocialmedia

Chapter 21

Meet Jenny G. Perry of
Peace, Love, Joy, & Sparkles

EVERY DAY FELT LIKE the movie *Groundhog Day,* and I was just going through the motions. It seemed like everything triggered a reaction within me. I was angry all the time about something. I was a victim of everything and everyone. I was a victim of my past. I was chock-full of regrets, brimming with self-judgment and shame.

I had already made myself a victim of my future, colored with fear, peppered with worry and stress. I was a victim of this world. I made myself a victim to life. I felt as if I had no power. I was so afraid of all the bad things that could happen. I was afraid to fully embrace life and to love with all of my heart. The idea of losing loved ones would overwhelm me. Frankly, I was a ball of anxiety.

I thought that if I lost weight, got a tummy tuck, won the lottery, the world was a nicer place, bad things didn't happen, people never judged me, everyone loved me, and had a nicer house, I'd be happy. I compared myself—and my life—with others. I didn't even know who I really was, unless I judged myself against another person. Everything was externally based. I felt as if I had no power to be happy, unless things outside of myself changed. I constantly tried to escape my reality. Holding my breath that my kids would grow up happy, healthy, and safe. Waiting to have my own life when they got older. Feeling like I missed out on a lot with getting married at 19 when I became pregnant with my daughter. I beat myself up daily, had a head full of judgment for myself and then judged others to make myself feel better. I felt that I was never going to be good enough. I felt like practically everyone I knew was better than me. I was convinced that too many things were wrong with me. I was a victim of myself. I was my own abuser.

I prayed for perspective without tragedy. I wanted to have a new outlook on my life. I desired to see all the good in everything, and I wanted to really appreciate my kids and all the blessings that I had, without having a tragedy to inspire a new understanding. I read spiritual books. I tried to a good Catholic. I also tried to immerse myself in new ideas and concepts. But my change didn't happen overnight. I just kept sliding in a different direction. Slowly, I'd grow, but in the end, I had to take a step back from everything and look within to get a clearer perspective.

Looking back at my childhood, I realized that I had always looked outside of myself for validation and love. I never felt good enough. I felt different, like I didn't fit in, unless someone liked me and gave me attention. Then I felt good. Only then did I feel special. I was embarrassed all the time and never felt like I could truly be myself. I felt like if people really knew me, they wouldn't like me.

I looked up to everyone else. I wanted to be everyone else. I felt like I was always one mistake away from not being loved by anyone. I had trouble sleeping, and every night I'd mentally fight with myself. I always felt like something bad was going to happen. I begged God not to let anything happen to my loved ones. I was fearful and anxious, and my mind was filled with worry. I'd pray for everything to be okay, but I continually played out fearful situations in my mind.

It's interesting to look back now, as I parent my four children and see how different they are from what I was. I thank God they are happy and don't have all that fear inside of them. You can't make a child have good self-esteem. They have to find it for themselves. I just try to give them a good foundation of love.

You can read every book out there on how to change your life. You can try to integrate the wisdom shared by others into your life. Yet, without looking within, nothing can change.

Your thoughts and feelings hold the key. That is what I began to learn. I had to stop and listen quietly. I'd ask: What was I telling myself? Was I listening to my mind chatter? These realizations sometimes were so subtle; I didn't realize to what extent my thoughts were running the show. I also began to discover that "my thoughts were not me."

Just because I had a passing thought didn't mean I had to keep it! I also learned that I didn't have to acknowledge every thought that passed through my brain.

Yes, I could think whatever I wanted. I could change my whole way of thinking. When I became aware of this, I thought, "Wow! This is free-

dom!" It also was terrifying. What scared me was the realization that I had to take responsibility for my life. I was studying *The Secret* by Rhonda Byrne and many other books on the Law of Attraction, including books from Abraham-Hicks. I was in transition, no longer sure how to be or how to live anymore. I was discovering that this new perspective was like being born into a whole new world—a world in which I could actually create myself! A "new me" was evolving every day, with each step—in each moment—a new frontier.

In time I began to realize that no matter how much my husband or mom—or *whoever*—loved me, it would be enough. I could not be rescued by anyone but myself. I had to rescue me. Someone could throw me a life preserver, but ultimately I had to choose to grab it and make it back to shore with my own strength. Finding the strength meant going deep within and looking at the parts of myself that I was afraid of or didn't want to accept. I had to let go of mistakes, forgive myself, and rebuild my self-esteem.

Being okay with *all* of myself led me to an epic and beautiful journey into self-love. I paid close attention to my feelings. I was getting better at observing and loving myself through the process. I was actually beginning to feel whether something was true or not, for me. I started to trust how I felt. My emotions and feelings were no longer the enemy. I learned that feeling good was natural, and I allowed myself to feel good even if things were not perfect. I could live in the now. Living in the moment was a mystery to me, and yet, it offered me an opportunity to explore and discover so many new insights. In the present moment, I could choose to feel good.

No matter how much money was in my bank account or what my kids were doing, I could feel good. I could *make a choice* to feel good. I began to realize that I had so much power—and surprisingly, it had existed within me all along! Knowing that I was always connected to this infinite, Divine Source of love and light transformed me.

It was a relief to know that I didn't need to be perfect in order to be awesome. I didn't need to be like anyone else, because there is no one else like me. Done with comparisons, I could decide what I wanted to be. I kept discovering who I was, and I began to create who *I wanted to be.*

I had to let go of what anyone, including myself, had ever thought of me. I had to let myself become the person I knew I truly was inside. Becoming me, as a powerful and vibrant woman, materialized as I shed the layers of what I was not. I had to release my intense fear of being judged or criticized. In the past, being as sensitive as I was, even the smallest comment felt like danger. I now knew that was just one way I was giving my power away to someone else. If I was going to be my *own* person, then no one else's opinion could matter more than my own. I had to let the self-love in.

I thought I would be judged by others for loving myself, but I took the leap anyway...and another leap...and another. I was committed to myself. No one, or no thing, outside of myself would complete me or make me whole. I complete me. I became my own best friend and soul mate.

Focusing on appreciating life—the lighter, happier, fun side of being alive—became my way of being. I realized I could enjoy life—and that when I do, then life changes in the process. I didn't have to change anything about myself except my thinking. My perspective was the lens through which I was seeing the world. I couldn't be happy until I chose to be happy. Happy thinking creates a happy life. I now understood that life was about the many choices that I made on a daily basis. Everything I chose—from what I watched on TV, the food I ate, the people I spent time with, and the activities I engaged in—were vital in creating a happy, empowered life. And yet, all of those kinds of choices paled in comparison to the importance of how I chose to think. My thoughts created everything in my life. I realized that I had the power to choose to put my attention on what I wanted, on things I liked, on good things, rather than on what I didn't want or things that I feared.

> "I realize that there are occasional benefits to staying a victim. It's easier to blame others for our misery. I have just learned that life is consistently more enjoyable as the victor."
>
> -Lori Rekowski
>
> facebook.com/FacesBehindThePages

I now understood that focusing on things that made me feel bad was a good indicator of how I was thinking. I had to think about things from the highest place within myself. And it was a joy to realize that even if I messed up, I could start again in each given moment. I could make many mistakes and mess things up and get off my path and go off in the wrong direction—and still love myself.

Everything was about perspective—how I was thinking, what I was focusing on—to create the energy that flowed through my life. When I stopped being so hard on myself, I stopped being so hard on everyone else. When I stopped judging myself so much, I stopped judging others so much. I became conscious of my power and how I could really let go and let God. I really started to get what God really meant for me. The journey was all about God and me, always.

As I bloomed more fully into myself, I realized that my deep connection to the Universe was personal—and collective. I could let others live their lives their way *and* I could live mine as I chose. Learning and experiencing that I was loved beyond measure—and that I was aware of my higher self—changed my life forever. Living from a higher place, with true intention, made me become whole.

Meditation became part of my routine. I focused with intention on really living life, not just watching on the sidelines. Living life "on purpose," with *intention*, full of love and light, became my basis for my new successful adventure of life.

I soon simplified my life. I stayed away from the news. I stayed out of other people's business. I didn't have to have an opinion on everything. I observed and dealt with, rather than *reacted*, to life. I didn't sweat the small stuff. I surrounded myself with positive people, steering clear of the negative ones. I am conscious of my energy field now, and I am deliberate about what I choose to focus on. Trusting my own guidance and enjoying the unfolding of who I become every day is now a bliss-filled adventure.

Now I'm free to be me. Life has become a place where I can play. I stop and smell the roses. I bask in what feels good. I do things that make me happy. The happier I am, the more it benefits my four kids. I choose me first. I choose to feel good, instead of trying to make everyone happy. This is impossible! I want to teach my kids that they are in charge of their own happiness. I want them to know that they have choices. They can choose to be happy. I've found that when you fill up your own love tank to the max, it overflows from your life to those around you. You become a blessing in their life when you are not "needing them" to be any different than they are. It is a gift to others—and yourself—when you stop imposing your will on others. It allows you to unconditionally love more freely.

Now, this doesn't mean that you can't set boundaries. Being clear with others is being loving when it is done in an honoring way. Life is so much sweeter when we stop living in the victim mode and step into our own personal power. We can love, live, and enjoy everything much more fully—especially ourselves.

Join me daily on my Facebook page:
http://www.facebook.com/peacelovejoysparkles
My website is *http://www.jennygperry.com*

Chapter 22

Meet Lisa Villa Prosen of *My Renewed Mind*

Why I Renew My Mind—My Sad Story

EVERYONE HAS ONE. You know it is true. We try to deny these sad stories, and for many this is where the trouble begins. They can be painful to acknowledge, and in my case, mine was crafted into the ultimate victim story.

I had a difficult childhood, plagued by divorce and I saw way too much for such a young girl. I learned at an early age that I could not drink like "normal" people. I was raised in a dysfunctional family, with generations of alcoholics, but I never knew that until much later in life. I just knew I was different from everyone else. None of them seemed as afraid and uncomfortable as I felt every day.

After leaving my home in Connecticut for life in the big city, I found some confidence in myself and worked as a bartender in Ft. Lauderdale, Florida. It was the eighties and drinking was still a lot of fun, but I eventually discovered cocaine. And as strange as it may sound, I am grateful that I did, since the progression of my decline was greatly accelerated. At the tender age of 22, I had used up all my drink tickets and I decided to stop taking all mood- or mind-altering drugs for good. Finding recovery at that age afforded me so many blessings and opportunities to change. I realized that, relatively speaking, I had not screwed up my life as much as other people I had met in sobriety.

The idea of reinventing me was fun. The people I met who were also recovering from alcoholism and drug addiction told me I had a fatal disease that was progressive in nature. I would forever remain an addict. The best I could hope for was a daily reprieve. I did as they suggested, I helped others, I found a higher power and I was on my way. Life became an amazing adventure.

I scoffed at the past and boldly embarked on the business of living a life beyond my wildest dreams. I made a bunch of money, bought a luxury car and a small home, and eventually married the man with whom I would spend the majority of my adult life. We raised our blended family while creating wealth and comfort that was indeed enviable.

Many years passed without thought of using drugs again. Over the years, I did have an occasional drink, and had convinced myself that I wasn't really an alcoholic. As long as I stayed away from drugs, I felt I would be okay. My life had changed so drastically from my previous life, my presobriety life in the bar business. Not only was I located in a different Florida city, I was a mother of five children, a very successful business owner, and living a typical upper-middle-class lifestyle in the suburbs. I was a *mom,* for goodness sake! I wouldn't even know where to begin to look for drugs now. I only drank on the rare occasions when I left the house for an evening with adults. So, for a time, the addiction seemed dormant. I thought I had dodged a bullet, that I was the exception.

As my children began to leave the nest, I wanted to work outside the home again. In 2007, after reading the *The Secret,* I was reminded of all that I had created in my youth. I felt recharged and decided to become a certified life success consultant, working directly with Bob Proctor and some of the most accomplished and relevant teachers in the world. I would train and inspire others to use the universal laws to their advantage. I worked during the days marketing and learning, coaching and consulting. However, as the U.S. economy began its decline, so did my wealth and my convictions.

My husband and I had amicably separated at the end of 2007, and the home I remained in with my two youngest children went into foreclosure. Our businesses were struggling, and no matter how positive I was, deep down I was becoming afraid. Retirement accounts were drained, insurance policies were cashed, and credit scores plummeted.

The straw that broke the camel's back was the news of my mother's stage-four cancer. I relapsed into oblivion, becoming unrecognizable to even my closest friends and family. The other recovering addicts were right about the progression.

This time, it was worse, much worse than before. I added compulsive gambling to my resume, and within a few months of going off the deep end, I got the call that my estranged husband had closed the doors of our business in my absence. Suddenly, I was dead *broke*. That was the fateful day when God decided to grace me with a moment of clarity. I chose to crawl home, with nothing left except the gift of desperation.

Okay, What Are You Selling?

In the course of an average life, every person is selling something. Sometimes we sell our sad stories, the payoff being empathy, sympathy, or depression. Sometimes we sell triumph over trials and adversity. Quite often, we peddle our woes and spend our time bonding with one another through our complaints about the way things are. We have become a society that loves our misery, and misery definitely loves company.

A few months into sobriety, I began to wonder how I could have fallen so far when I knew so much. The bottom line was that in order to move forward, I had to find balance between intellect and spirit. I knew that in order to transform my life, I had to be vigilant about remembering and applying this information in my life. I spent a lot of time on Facebook, reconnecting with my old school friends. It is important to mention that I never wanted to be the kind of personal development trainer who took herself too seriously. I had many professional contacts from my time as a coach, but I was not sure how that part of my life would pan out going forward.

There were many inspiring quotes appearing on this ever-evolving social network. I was collecting them in a photo album on my personal page. This seemed to be a real trend. I thought I would create my own space to display what inspired me personally. My Renewed Mind was born. It began as a venue for reading about the uplifting ideals that had worked and continued to work in my life . . . until I could figure out what was next. I contemplated my future and applied all that I knew without reservation. I admit that I still struggle to meditate daily, but I also remember that one should strive for progress, not perfection. My Renewed Mind is a place to have fun, be inspired, and provoke thought to cause positive changes in life.

I never felt right positioning myself as an expert in the field of coaching, consulting, or teaching. I felt like a fake, and hypocrisy was no stranger to me. The more time I spent around the "successful" coaches and speakers, the more I realized I did not want to be like them. A certain "used-car salesman" vibe always seemed to emanate from their podiums. They lacked the sincerity and personal touch that I wanted to use as the model for my business. On the other hand, there were also the healers and intuitives. These spiritually gifted ones had all the personal connection I was attracted to, but as far as I could tell, they weren't living the way I wanted to live.

We see what we are ready to see, I guess. My beliefs about money and financial abundance have changed considerably since then, but I mention this to illustrate my conundrum. I wanted a business model that would allow me to earn a comfortable living that didn't leave me feeling like I was selling snake oil. Using the universal principals, including the law of attraction, I contemplated my future every day. Gradually, the way became clear, and people were attracted to my writing on My Renewed Mind. What had originated as a tool to help me remember why I was here had become a community that allowed me to live my purpose. Those whom I am meant to help will get a feel for my straight-forward approach in advance.

I am a Go-Through Not a Guru

Brilliance and goodness are in all of us. I approach my clients with the premise that they are already whole, already perfect. I now realize through my own spiritual journey that everything that continues to resonate within me is simply what I need to remember. I was never learning or teaching; it was all a process of remembering what I am here to accomplish. Each day is another opportunity to practice living from that mentality.

If anyone did to me what I did to myself, I would have had a case for justifiable homicide. There was no way for me to learn what I now realize except to go through it. All of it.

It has been said that we are souls inhabiting physical bodies. My soul is most alive when I share my truth with the world. I have been astonishingly blessed by many wonderful people who remind me how my relationship with the truth helps them have the courage to share their deepest fears and break through them once and forever.

We are always remembering and practicing. I remember that love is all that truly lasts forever. I have realized that there are others who share the sensitivity of spirit that once caused me to feel that I was different. I am an empath. I have remembered how to listen to the nudging of my creator while trusting that I must guard myself from the destructive influence of psychic vampires. I use this gift to relate to others and see through the masks of fear and resentment. I plug in to the source of all creation and ask for clear thinking. I thank God for another day, another chance to be my authentic self. Today, I surround myself with other people that "get me" and support me in my unlimited potential. I am aware that I can help other people in a powerful way, and I do not have to be perfect to do that. What a relief.

There are many paths to home. I possess no magical fairy dust. Trusting that I have been brought to this place in my life for a really good reason has also been a process. My mother's cancer is in remission. Thank you, God. My life is once again moving in a direction that honors the grace I have been shown. I wake up (almost) every day with joyous anticipation for what I can accomplish and remember. I am useful and whole. My instincts, once gone completely awry, have returned to something that resembles sanity. Instincts, faith, and My Renewed Mind are my biggest assets today. I look forward to meeting you as we journey through this physical life together.

I give a special thank you to all the abundance-minded page owners who have helped My Renewed Mind grow and prosper by sharing my posts on your pages. We are truly a partnership in spreading good will and hope. Each of us serves a purpose; there is a glove for every hand. There is a quote for every doubt.

 Lisa Villa Prosen is an accomplished author, coach, speaker, and certified life success consultant. She has considerable experience in the fields of addiction recovery and personal development. A passionate promoter of self-empowerment and proud steward of a blended family, Lisa specializes in assisting others in remembering the source of their own power, and in so doing, helping them build their own bridges from painful pasts to brighter, more rewarding futures. Presently, Lisa shares her potent blend of wisdom and compassion in her Facebook page, My Renewed Mind. It is there that the uninitiated and the "expert" alike can benefit from Lisa's ability to distill complex metaphysical and spiritual principles into easily understandable and relatable truths based on actual life experience.

http://www.facebook.com/myrenewedmind
http://lisaprosen.com/

Positive Feedback from Her Readers:

"A friend of mine sent me a link to one of your posts and I have been receiving your posts ever since. I just wanted to let you know how much I appreciate and find your posts so uplifting."

"I have been battling PTSD and Bulimia for 4 years now and the encouragement and enlightenment that your posts have given me daily is

amazing. My mum said to me today that she has noticed a huge improvement in me recently and straight away I replied that I'm helped by my renewed mind."

"Thank you for helping me stay strong. It is a truly selfless and lovely thing that you spare the time to help keep the rest of us uplifted daily."

"You are an inspiration! You give a lot of yourself for others and I enjoy your daily posts , we are not alone and doing the best we can and that's what counts ,one day at a time for me and my sobriety prayer has got me to levels in my life I have never seen , very happy with my life and know how to keep it that way no matter bad days are few and far between now compared to me over 4 years ago , god bless and tk you :) xo"

"Lisa . . . thank you for sharing this. Thank you for letting us in. Thank you for letting others know they aren't alone. Thanks for letting *me* know I'm not alone when it comes to having a problem with procrastinating."

Chapter 23

Meet Bernard Alvarez of the
Global Illumination Council

I NEVER LIKED THIS WORLD. As a child I always felt like an observer looking in on a tragic play. Kids were mean to one another, grown-ups argued, and the TV news always scared me. While I was lucky enough to have a two-parent household, all the kids in the neighborhood had divorced parents. This is not to say I had an unhappy childhood; on the contrary, as an only child adopted into a childless home, I was the world to my parents and they never left me in want of anything.

Yet I never seemed to feel like I belonged here. I was never able to fully grasp the whole "normal" life that was portrayed on TV and in the homes of my childhood friends. Family gatherings were a burden and distraction. Sports and other team activities were forced on me by my family and friends. All the while I just wanted to write or read and be left alone to my thoughts. And what beautiful thoughts they were. Thoughts and daydreams of beautiful exotic places, scenes of a utopian land filled with smiling children, dancing grown-ups and beautiful animals roaming freely. I guess one could say I dreamed of and longed for my own personal Eden.

My youth was what one might call misspent. I grew up very quickly once I became a teenager and experienced many of the things one might not have until their college years. I was a wild child, to my parents' disappointment, but my consistent above-average grades, academic awards, and honors gave my parents little room to complain or punish me. So I was a genius party boy by age 15 and graduated high school with honors at the age of 16. The world was mine to experience and my teenage ego and fawning parents made me a bit of a spoiled brat and an intellectual snob. I thought I was the best and demanded the best clothes, cars, friends, beautiful lovers, experiences, and surroundings.

When I was seventeen I dropped out of university and pursued a career in the fashion world as a stylist and part-time model. I thought I had it made. Lots of money (way too much for someone that young and irresponsible), plenty of luxuries, parties, red-carpet affairs, multiple lovers, complimentary country club memberships, and being in Miami during the rebirth of South Beach offered plenty of mind-altering substances in abundance. I was a rock star in my own mind and to my wealthy clientele and business contacts.

This lifestyle continued through my twenties and some of my thirties, but it wasn't as easy to enjoy. You see, when I was in my early twenties I discovered pagan and shamanic spirituality. This discovery led me down a path of remembrance and spiritual awakening. I sought out teachers and took classes, read every book on metaphysics and the occult I could get my hands on, and eventually had a full-fledged shamanic vision quest. As one of my mentors once said, my chakras were blown wide open and I was too young or not ready for the information I received. My whole outlook on life and my identity were challenged from that day on. Self-interest was suddenly an ugly concept, materialism and luxury an unnecessary expense, violence and manipulation a sign of weakness. I had awoken to my higher self and made contact with my spirit guides.

One of the first lessons I learned from my teachers was that a true shaman has his foot on every plane of existence and can alter one's state of consciousness at will. This is something I would struggle with for the next fifteen years. By day I was a superstar stylist catering to the wealthy and catered to by the elite in my community, and by night I was a pseudomystic taking classes, getting certifications in Reiki, the magical arts, and metaphysics. Eventually, I would go on to become a spiritual teacher at my Unitarian church and multiple metaphysical and new age shops around town, all the while living a parallel life as a rock star stylist and all that it entailed.

For a time in the late nineties and early twenty-first century I was a popular personality in my city. I became an ambassador of the city's chamber of commerce, hosted exclusive VIP parties at the local clubs, never having to pay for a meal or a drink at the local restaurants and bars. The local politicians and police officers knew me by name, making it easy for me to get away with lots of things no one else could, including having a police car escort me home if I had a bit too much to drink. Again I found myself a spoiled brat. Eventually, I was asked to run my own salon in an exclusive area of Miami and I thought I had made it. Life was good and I was on top of the world. Then suddenly, it all began to fall apart.

In October 2005 Hurricane Wilma blew through South Florida with the force of an atomic bomb. I remember we hadn't thought it would hit so hard and all of my windows were left exposed to the elements. I watched in terror as I saw our wooden fence ripped from the ground and fly two blocks away like it was a piece of paper. A tornado had come between our house and the neighbors, making its way to the backyard and sucking up a bolted steel garden shed and tossing it into the road. I held my two cats under each arm as we cowered in the hall, ready to climb under the mattress I had placed on the bathtub should the windows break and we needed to take cover. As the roaring sound of the winds and snapping trees continued, I knew my life would never be the same.

The next day I awoke to another world. Paradise was now in tatters and resembled a war zone. Cars and trucks were crushed by roofs and trees that had blown on them. Miraculously, my little convertible suffered no damage parked between two palm trees. My mobile phone still worked and I received a call from an employee to turn on the local news. As I gazed blankly at the news report my eyes were astonished by the scene being transmitted into my home. The local news had captured footage of my salon's storefront exploding onto the street. I saw shampoo bottles, magazines, and brushes rolling down the avenue and rain pouring into the shop. My heart dropped. My dreams had literally been blown away.

From there it was a fast descent into poverty and virtual homelessness. My clientele began to dwindle as I was forced to work from my home. Those who once celebrated me in my community disappeared. Eventually I was illegally evicted and forced to move into a friend's home. It was there where I began to share my story on YouTube where it was quickly picked up and featured on Sky News. I continued to make videos and was made one of the first partners on YouTube which helped me gain exposure and fame quickly on the video circuit.

I believe the first lessons I learned from my experience was that sincerity, honesty, and integrity are not negotiable in my world. Business is not just business, status is not power and those who aren't there for us through the rough patches are not real friends. This is something I carried over onto my next project after gaining notoriety on YouTube.

In 2007, while still couch hopping from friend to friend's homes, I started doing an Internet radio program called EKBTV LIVE. We mostly covered corruption in government or what some may consider "truther" topics. The show also included metaphysical topics such as the law of attraction, personal empowerment, and other tools to overcome adversity. Then I had my second awakening.

Some may call it a lucid dream, a hallucination, or just poppycock, but I know better. One morning while still on my friend's couch, I was awakened by a voice in my head that kept repeating three words to me: Global Illumination Council. I had no idea what to make of it, only that I knew I had to let the EKBTV project go and move forward with this "Global Illumination Council" project, whatever that would be. I awoke feeling very refreshed and like myself again. If this can make sense, I felt like I did when I was fifteen. Not jaded or angry or hostile anymore, but rather feeling very open, trusting, and peace-filled. It was as if my spirit knew that after the last year of tragedy I would be taken care of, not by me or my elitist fake friends, but by the universe itself. I was wholly me again.

The following year I teamed up with a spiritual life coach to co-host my radio show, and I launched an Internet TV station to play empowering documentaries and my videos. While co-hosting with me she discovered that I had begun writing a book in the early nineties that had lessons from my shamanic vision quest. She immediately began encouraging me to complete the book and volunteered to transcribe the entire book for submission. We eventually self-published it and *The Book of One* was born.

With a popular YouTube channel, Internet TV, and radio stations we needed a place to bring it all together. It was a fluke. I sat down in front of the computer one night and discovered a social networking platform and then next thing you know Global Illumination Council was live. Finally we had a place to share our many projects with the public, in one place. I had written a lovely petition a year earlier and we turned it into the now popular GIC pledge. Little by little people from around the planet began to find us and call us home. We had created an oasis for seekers of truth, empowerment, social justice, whistle-blowers, light workers, pagans, new agers, and activists.

Today we have over 4,000 official members globally with over 30,000 fans on our Facebook page and continue to offer all our programs for free. GICTV, GIC Radio, and our YouTube channel are continuing to share the message of humanity's awakening through personal empowerment. I have a wonderful team of volunteer administrators and content creators who work passionately for the movement. I can't say that I have made much money from all of this work but I have learned that sometimes having enough to do what we love is what matters most. Live your bliss. Follow your intuition, always.

 Dr. Bernard Alvarez D.M. is a producer, author, activist, visionary, founder of the Global Illumination Council, YouTube partner, radio personality, consciousness teacher, and social critic. He has been a spiritual teacher for over twenty years. He is a certified Reiki master, an ordained minister, has a doctor of metaphysics, is the author of the *Book of One*. He's produced and published hundreds of teaching videos and has appeared on TV and dozens of radio shows.

Bernard is currently the empowerment director of the Global Illumination Council (an international spiritual activist network) and the host of all GIC network TV and Radio shows. He also continues to write and publish spiritual teaching videos and series on the GIC YouTube Partner channel.

As an activist, Bernard sees that there must be a balance in creating outward change as well as internal spiritual change. He is an advocate for global justice and is involved in the international Occupy movement, and is also a facilitator for his local Occupy Roanoke.

Bernard currently lives in Roanoke, Virginia, with his two cats, Isis and Sofia.

http://www.facebook.com/justbernard
http://www.facebook.com/GlobalIlluminationCouncil

Chapter 24

Meet Anne Nyambura Mwangi of
The Age of Women

The Age of Women

THE AGE OF WOMEN is a page that is inspired by a teaching of the same name from the teachings of Marshall Vian Summers. It calls for the rise of women in areas of leadership, particularly in the areas of religion and spirituality, for leaders must be providers and maintainers. The Age of Women is not here to replace men and men should also not be threatened by this, for it is an assumption of natural abilities. The page was created to act as a wake-up call for these women and for the men who will play a part in the rise of the age of women, for there are many women today in the world who are destined to be great leaders and are currently living a life far below what they were meant to live, and their gifts and contribution will never come to fruition in this lifetime if they do not wake up and become the people who they are destined to become. The page also brings forth a teaching about a deeper intelligence, a perfect guiding intelligence that is in all sentient beings in the universe. For all sentient beings are born with two minds, a mind to think with and a mind to know. The mind to think with is the personal mind, but the mind to know is the knowing mind and this is the source of spirituality in the universe.

The face behind the Facebook page of the Age of Women is not the face of one person, for there are many faces that will follow, but it is currently being run and maintained by one person. More important than my story are the lessons that I have learned during my time here on earth, which instead of putting it in a narrative form, I have taken the lessons and the solutions that I found to maneuver my way out of these challenges and presented them in another perspective. There is also another challenge that I face still, and I face it everyday. It comes from following the teachings of *Steps to Knowledge: The Book of Inner Knowing*, a book that is presented online for free which is a one-year self-study course. This has been by far the biggest challenge that has taken me to my limits and beyond, for in taking this course, I find that I have to keep on facing myself each day and that is far more confronting and far more difficult and far more painful than anything I have ever done in my life, because now, I am dealing with myself. Taking the Steps to Knowledge is building a foundation for the emergence of this deeper power in one's life. All the great saints and poets and musicians and those who have brought about substantial change and improvement for humanity have known of this, have practiced this. It is not enough to say that they were uniquely endowed individuals who had almost superhuman patience and courage to carry on such great works, for this power and courage resides within all of us and it is called knowledge. But first we must create a place for it within ourselves. As it is said in one of the teachings:

The foundation is so very important and requires great patience and forbearance. It is this patience and forbearance that will shift your allegiance away from your intellect and the admonitions of others to a Greater Power within you—the power of Knowledge, the power of God. You will never comprehend this powerfully. You can never claim it for yourself. You

will never be a master of it. You can never use it to try to be better than oth-ers. You cannot use it to get what you want. You cannot use it to gain wealth and power and pleasure. You can only learn to follow it and learn of the great journey up the mountain that was always prepared for you.
    —*Building a Bridge to a New Life*

So this is my story, written from another perspective.

The Pressure Law

It simply states that the pressure of a gas of a fixed volume is directly proportional to its temperature. No, this article is not about physics, but if you have ever bottled up your feelings inside until you exploded and left a behind a trail of destruction, then you know more about the pressure law than you give yourself credit for. The people pleaser, the one who never wants to hurt other people's feelings or keeps silent for the sake of peace while others walk all over them, those stressed from their labors who have no creative vent while all the time the pressure is building up inside are like physicists building an atomic bomb in their minds without knowing it.

Physics 101 to all the Members of the Emotional Manhattan Project

A controlled reaction is a nuclear power plant. It is useful in that it can be used to generate electricity at affordable prices. The disadvantage is the nuclear waste, but if disposed of correctly, it can have minimal harm to the environment.

An uncontrolled reaction is an atomic bomb: It is messy and leaves behind untold casualties and the effects reach out far into the future.

Take a piece of paper and create beautiful poetry, buy some paint and create beautiful art, run a marathon, take up boxing, cycling, or dancing, or just doodle something on a piece of paper. No one wants a nuclear reaction but when you have it, then the energy in the emotional nuclear power plant is neutral. You can use it, or you can abuse it.

Beloved Past Times

A victim has two favorite pastimes—throwing free pity parties and going on all-expense-paid guilt trips, the cost of which is their spiritual, emotional, and sometimes physical health, and in some extreme cases, relationships. The key problem is the reply button on the remote control of their lives, which they constantly hit, basking in their victimization and the attention they get from others, while walking around as if everyone owes them something because of the extent of their suffering. If there is anyone who tolerates that in your life, then rest assured they will not be there for long and if they do stay, then when you change and become empowered they will leave you.

A Traveler's Guide out of Victimization

Step One: *Forgive yourself.* So you do not think that you did anything worth deserving to be forgiven by your self or anyone. It was others who hurt you, but the truth is people only have as much power over your life as you allow them to have. So forgive yourself for allowing others or circumstances to hurt you.

Step Two: *Forgive others.* For in truth, if you sincerely take the time to understand their circumstances, you will realize in most cases, they did their best with the knowledge and understanding that they possessed at that particular moment. When you understand this, do not throw another pity party or go on another guilt trip, but go back to step one.

Step Three: *Understand yourself.* See that the guilt trips are a way of punishing yourself for some unknown misdemeanor. Get to the root of the problem and stop treating the symptoms. Some of the roots go far back into the childhood stages and the sooner you understand it, the sooner you can deal with it and remove work through the experience, once and for all, instead of repeating the same old cycles. In most cases, you may have to repeat steps two and one.

Step Four: *Learn to communicate properly.* See that the pity parties are a miscommunication of your situation to others and, in many cases, a call for assistance from others. A pity party often drains people of their energy and in turn they can have none left for you. Compose yourself, sit down and meditate, and consider your words before communicating with others.

The Prison without Bars

Others leave their victim mentality and having strayed into unfamiliar territory, they fall back into the old mind patterns that are comforting and do not require much effort. They still have the same script but with different casts. In essence, they have left one prison and entered another. It may be new and exciting, but it is still the same old conditions. So a cycle of imprisonment and illusion of freedom begins, where stimulation is sought in new and exciting experiences, which in essence, when viewed objectively, are no different from one another. Worse still, those stuck in these cycles are unable or unwilling to perceive these cycles because they do not have the courage to choose their freedom.

Jail Break

Watch your mind, watch what you tell yourself. Yes, this is a lot of work, but you never did this before, and look at where it has gotten you. The mind was created to be creative and it will create; even to its own destruction, even to its detriment, it is creative. It is like fire, a loyal servant but a cruel master. You are the only one who can determine the role that it will play. You either tame it or it will rule you.

The Mighty High Horse

There could never be greater evidence of insecurity than that which makes anyone believe they are above others. Trying to prove that you are better than others is evidence that something is lacking in your life, for if nothing was lacking, then others would be uplifting because you would have a surplus.

Dismounting

Those who fall off their high horses inevitably land on mirrors. Love and respect yourself enough to spare yourself the shock, pain, and embarrassment. Recognize that this is in reality avoiding your real situation. You judge others before they judge you, believing the world to be harsh and cruel, because the alternative is that you will have to deal with your own shortcomings. You are avoiding; otherwise you would have to take a good look at yourself and that is far more painful than the harsh, cruel, and judgmental world.

How We Love to Hate Them

They have the Midas touch. Everything they touch flourishes, they have successful careers, happy partnerships, and talented children. They are beautiful and admired by many, and how we love to hate them and smirk at their downfall. This is insecurity in disguise.

Honor Your Path

Honor and respect your path in life and do not look at others or their paths, save to assist them to the best of your ability (if they are in need of such assistance) and to learn the important lessons that they are there to teach. The only path that you can ever take is your own and should you ever take it on yourself to walk in another's path, the best you will ever become is second best.

The White Knight

Disney gave you an unrealistic expectation of love. The white knight saved Snow White, rescued Cinderella just before he kissed Sleeping Beauty and you have since been waiting for him to come and tell you how beautiful you are, and give you all your sense of self-worth. No one can do this for you. If there is anyone like that in your life, then start marking your calendar, because it is a matter of time before they leave.

You will drain them of all their energy because you will ask for more than they can give.

You Are the Saviour You Have Been Waiting For

Stand in front of the mirror today and say, "I love you" and repeat this the following day and repeat this until you truly and unconditionally love, honor, and respect yourself. If you cannot get your sense of self-worth from yourself, then you will not get it from anyone else. Anyone who has the power to give you the illusion that they can give you a sense of self-worth can use and abuse it as they please. Never is a victim more vulnerable than when they are waiting for a saviour.

Fear and All Its Friends

Fear leads to avoidance, which leads to addictions, which leads to excuses, and inevitably, to failure. Does that mean that people should get rid of fear? Fear is neutral. Under good measure, it can be seen as caution. It is caution that makes you go to work, because if you do not, you will not be able to pay the bills. It is caution that tells you to eat healthy, because if you do not, you will become ill. It is caution that tells you not to accept gifts from strangers or let strangers in your house, because if you do, it may not turn out well. So it is unwise to say that you will get rid of fear. However, irrational fear is destructive and can paralyze you and your activities.

First Steps to Freedom

Step 1: *Do not procrastinate.* Once you procrastinate, you enter a comfort zone. The longer you are in the comfort zone, the more difficult it will be for you to leave it.

Step 2: *Watch your addictions.* Behavioral addictions are repetitive forms of behavior that occupy the time which would otherwise be spent constructively. Ask yourself, what would you do if you were not preoccupied with certain activities, and you may learn a great deal about yourself.

Step 3: *Identify your excuses.* Excuses are like the get-out-of-jail-free cards. When making excuses, you never get to the root cause and always remain at the surface. Never treat the symptoms. That is like weeding the garden by cutting out the stems but leaving the roots intact.

The Teacher and the Stone

A woman was once brought in front of a teacher by a mob that wanted to stone her because of her deeds. The teacher then told the mob that the one without sin should be the one to cast the first stone and they all walked away and there was no one left to stone her. Do not be ashamed of your mistakes, but rejoice in the lessons that they taught you. Do not allow others to make you feel ashamed of your mistakes, for none is above making mistakes. Do not console yourself by telling yourself that there are others who are in a worse situation than you are. Let not the misfortunes of others be a source of solace for you.

Find your inner strength. Be like the tree whose roots are deep in the soil and can fare in all weather.

 A human rights activist, an environmentalist, an artist who uses her skills to educate others and a student of Steps to Knowledge, a study course based on the teachings of Marshall Vian Summers:

"Steps to Knowledge does not require that you worship any hero or any personality. It does not require that you accept a creation story about life that is implausible and impossible. It does not require that you believe in a pantheon of gods, images, symbols, rituals, pageants or personalities. It only brings you to the great question of what you really know. And it does not answer this question in words, but instead takes you into the experience of Knowledge itself, slowly, through many steps and stages of development."

https://www.facebook.com/TheAgeOfWomen
http://www.newmessage.org/nmfg/The_New_Message_from_God.html

Chapter 25

Meet Lisa K. Fox, Psychic Medium

WHEN I WAS JUST 4 years old, I accompanied my parents one summer day as they went to explore the immense and amazing Bandelier National Park in Los Cruces, New Mexico.

Home to ancestral pueblo Indians, such as the Anasazi, its limestone rock cliffs are pocketed with hundreds of cave dwellings carved directly into the soft limestone. Each home has a small hole in the floor called a "Spirit hole," which allowed their loved ones in Spirit to freely come and go.

My parents and I climbed down a simple, angled, wooden ladder into a huge meeting room called the "Ceremonial Kiva." It was very dark and cool, lit only by a slant of sunlight beaming through the square opening above our heads.

As I turned around, the room was filled with dark faces speaking a language I didn't understand. They were laughing, singing, and smiling over at me, and the room was smoky from the fire in the center. I pinned myself up against the curved wall and ran over to my father.

"Daddy! There are people in here—and we are in their house!"

I didn't bring this up again until only a year ago, and my dad said he recalled the incident perfectly. When I asked him what he said to me, he replied with a wry smile, "Oh, I told you I believed you...."

Thus began my adventures with the dead.

For many years growing up I felt like a freak, seeing and hearing spirits and knowing things that no one else did.

I felt like I had a satellite on my head that picked up information that nobody else could receive, a flow I could never turn off. My dad once told me that my maternal Irish grandma was psychic, and he called her a "white witch." She did readings for people with simple playing cards, but the day she foretold her own mother's death—and then her mother died—she stopped using her gifts altogether.

At the age of 19, I was in college visiting a friend in her dorm room. She had a new book that taught you how to tell fortunes with playing cards, and thought it would be fun for us to try it out. The moment my hands touched the cards, I went into a trance and uttered things to her, many of which later came true.

I had no memory of this and became quite frightened by what was happening to me. I went to the library and researched as much as I could. I became even more scared when I realized there were actual terms for what I was doing. I read about extrasensory perception, clairvoyance, and other psychic abilities. My friends at the time thought it was fun, and I started to feel like a party favor in demand by people who wanted me to entertain them. Not unlike other psychics who came before me, I felt absolutely cursed and began to ignore Spirits and anything else that came to me. I just wanted it all to go away.

At 22, I became a Christian and asked God to please take these horrible abilities away from me and turn my curse into something beautiful, like the "gifts of the Spirit" I had learned about as a girl.

I just wanted to be useful to God, and somehow bring healing to others, if I could. I had no idea how to do that. I was placed in the prayer room during church services, because I was told that I had "the gift of discernment."

Finally! I could be of use and serve God in this way. I had a place, and didn't feel like a freak.

My son was born about ten years later, weighing in at 12 pounds, 14 ounces, and 22 inches long. I had him naturally, because no one had a clue how big he really was.

I lost so much blood during childbirth that I lost consciousness and floated out of my body towards a beautiful huge orb of light. I met someone there who told me it wasn't my time and that I needed to go back. I felt such love and peace, happy to be away from the excruciating pain of the birth. But I didn't want to go back. I felt hands on my shoulders, and they turned me around, and I heard, "Look down." I saw my son, covered in blood being worked on, and my body lifeless on the bed. I said, "I can't leave my baby," and instantly I was back in my body flooded with pain. During this ordeal, I heard unearthly singing like I'd never heard before; later, I figured that I must been hearing angels. There wasn't a dry eye in that hospital room that night. Everyone knew that something miraculous had just happened.

Shortly after this incredible near-death experience, I once again began hearing and seeing spirits very clearly. My abilities were back with a vengeance. It was getting harder and harder to ignore what was coming to me. I visited my ancestral home of Ireland and had more experiences with Spirits. In an 11th century chapel, I placed my hands on the rough-hewn stonework and was startled to hear monks chanting and singing for a few moments.

I never trusted the information I received. I never believed that I was truly psychic or had any special abilities—but I wanted to believe that I maybe I was.

Everyone around me—my partners, my friends, and even some family members—would make fun of me and even put me down. I was told that I was "crazy" and that I was a "psychic in training." I may have lacked self-confidence, but I knew that I had something that I could use in honor of God, something that I could use to help heal people. If only I could just connect with it and understand it.

I met my meditation teacher in 2007, and I began to meditate every Tuesday night with a small group of people. I learned about my chakras and how to connect not only with my own body's energy, but the highest vibrations of the universe. I learned to do hands-on healing, and I began to read everyone and everything around me with incredible accuracy. My ability to see, hear and sense everything was off the charts.

Spirits began coming to me in droves, asking for my help.

My meditation teacher taught me to not be afraid, that most of those coming to me were wandering souls who didn't even understand that they were dead. She explained that I was incredibly gifted and could help them by listening and sharing their messages with their loved ones here on the Earth plane. She also said I could offer the light to these wandering souls, should they be ready to cross over, if they wanted and needed to go.

Soon I realized that they were still people—just without their human form. They deserved my love and my compassion just as if they were still here in the flesh. I realized that I finally had a way to help, a way to heal. My curses became blessings. I was both terrified and overwhelmed at first, but with much practice I began to do my first in-person readings. I had the love and support of my entire meditation group, which told me I could do this work and cheered me on.

At home, however, it was a different story. The person with whom I was in relationship was antagonistic about my gifts. I was belittled and constantly put down. I received no support or acknowledgment of who I was. Still, I pressed on—trusting that there was more to this experience; there had to be a reason why I was given these abilities.

When I started to read for others, incredible and amazing things began to happen. People's lives were changed, and souls on the other side were able to share their messages of love with my clients. Such an incredible healing was taking place, not only for my clients, but also for the souls of their loved ones who now existed in Spirit on the other side of the veil. We all felt so much clarity and peace. I was astonished—being a vessel for Spirit. I learned to just get out of the way and let Spirit move and do its work through me. Spirit communicated and got the job done in whatever way was needed. I just had to believe. I just had to trust and surrender to my gift.

People who didn't support me, those who were toxic in my life, fell away immediately, because my eyes were fixed on being of service to the universe—no matter what. I was determined to continue growing and developing my gifts, because I saw that I could help heal souls, one at a time, both on this side of the veil and on the other.

My Facebook page was an outpouring of that transformation.

I wanted to make myself accessible to people so that they could understand how Spirit works, so that they could do as I have done and follow in the footsteps of a real psychic medium. I answered their questions, and they responded. They told me that my readings were life changing, and they shared how much comfort and peace came to them. Whether it was a psychic reading or a post that I put up on my page, I was completely amazed at how Spirit was moving through me.

I really had no knowledge of how to run a Facebook page. I just put myself out there. I shared experiences about my pain, my joy, my suffering and my personal experiences in Spirit.

Every time I wrote a story about a Spirit, people became so excited and wanted more. They encouraged me and loved when I gave free readings on my page. My experience on Facebook continued to grow far beyond my wildest imagination. I never dreamt in a million years that I would have so many fans who would love and support me and look for inspiration in my daily posts. Just one comment made my entire day or week.

I continue to reach out to people—one soul at a time—so that they know how much they are loved and cared for—not only by me, but by their loved ones in Spirit, and by their angels and guides. I want to show them that there is so much more to this life experience than what we can see, hear or feel. I want them to know that their loved ones in Spirit are never really truly gone, because they continue to love and watch over them always.

So many people have told me how blessed they are that I share my gift with others now. I continue to just bask in the love of Spirit. It is an incredible honor and privilege to share my gifts with the world to help heal and bring peace, comfort, and clarity, whatever is needed, one person at a time and one soul at a time.

I'm Lisa K. Fox and I AM a clairvoyant psychic Medium.

 Lisa is an internationally known and respected clairvoyant psychic medium. She is fully certified and endorsed by world renowned psychic medium Lisa Williams, and is a Spiritual Advisor on her website "Soul Connections" (*www.soulconnections.com*).

Lisa is a very gifted fifth generation medium, who has the honor of bringing often life changing messages from your loved ones in Spirit for comfort, healing, clarity and peace.

Lisa gives spiritually based psychic guidance, helping to empower you in finding your highest and best path along with your own intuitive gifts. She covers every aspect of your soul's journey past, present and future. She is also a gifted medical intuitive, animal communicator and healer.

Chapter 26

Meet Bex Gibbons of *Your Inner Sparkle*

LIKE MANY OTHERS, I have had my fair share of ups and downs in this lifetime. When I look back on the past thirty-four years of my life, I wonder how I managed to hold it together at all. How I possibly found the strength to continue on in the face of adversity, I really do not know. It seems this journey that I had planned for myself would be filled with many experiences, ultimately helping me to grow with much strength and wisdom.

After being adopted at birth and my adoptive dad dying when I was 4, my adoptive mother remarried my biological grandfather, who destroyed my world even more by sexually abusing me for many years. I finally escaped at age 12 when I managed to get away to boarding school for five years. However, at school I was bullied for being weird and abnormal, and I found myself discouraged, alone and fighting bulimia. I finally got out on my own at 18 and started to make my way in this world.

I remembered all the feelings like they had happened just yesterday, feeling so abandoned and unloved and alone, but I kept struggling forward in the hope that one day my life would somehow turn around, and I would be happy for the first time in a very long time. I met my husband-to-be, and finally, for the first time, I felt loved and wanted and needed. By this stage of my life, I had tried to mask my sadness with drugs and alcohol and had fallen into a cycle of even more self-destruction. I thank my children every day for giving me a reason to clean up my act and be sober and healthy to bring them both into the world.

Not long after my second child was born, I fell into a very deep depression and a lot of old feelings came up to the surface. I decided that it was time to put the man who brought so much hurt, distrust, and emotional turmoil into my life behind bars to pay for what he had done. I decided that I was going to choose more than to just survive. I was not going to be a victim anymore. I was not going to live the abuse day in and day out for the rest of my life, feeling afraid and paranoid of any male that came close to my children. My abuser was sentenced to jail for only eleven months, and I fell apart quicker than I ever could have expected. I packed my bags and decided that was it. Nothing about my life was worth living for. I told myself that my kids were better off without me as I was nothing but a horrible person and mother. I took off into the night looking for the first power pole to launch my car into, because in my mind, life was just that bad and I couldn't do it anymore!

Someone was definitely watching over me that night, because something inside of me just kept telling me to turn around and go home, that it would be okay, and that I just needed to hold on a little longer. So I drove home and promptly called a counselor the next day. To my surprise, a week later I was diagnosed with rapid cycling bipolar disorder and admitted to an outpatient treatment unit. They tried every drug in the book on me—ones that turned me into a walking zombie, others that made all my hair fall out, and still others that almost stopped me from functioning at all. Not one person acknowledged the circumstances that led up to this or what I had been dealing with for many, many years. I was promptly stuck into a category and left to my own devices. Six very long months down the track, I decided that it was time for me to take my life back, to be my own hero, to stand up for myself, and to begin to love myself again, something that I hadn't been able to do in a very, very long time. This was the pivot point in my life, a time that I will forever hold close to my heart. This was the time where I found the courage to step up and find the happiness in my life that I so longed for, to find the love within me that I knew was always there but that I had never taken the time to nurture. This was my time. I was determined to make it happen, and that is exactly what I did.

Now I can say, after making my way through all of these life lessons, that I am thankful for each and every one of them, because if it were not for these experiences, I never would have found my way into the amazing spiritual community of amazing people on Facebook that I did. I watched this community as it uplifted me and nurtured me, surrounding me in love and positivity every day. I decided that if I could help just one other person see the light at the end of the tunnel, if just one of my experiences brought the words that were so needed by just one other person to feel better, to help them find their way, to bring them a smile, to let them know they are loved and not alone, then I knew I would have done my part. However small it was, I just knew in my heart that the ripples would be great.

That was the thinking behind my page, and in that moment Your Inner Sparkle was born. For the first week, I never shared my page or let anyone know it existed. I was simply too scared to be judged and made fun of so I held back until the very same Reiki master who initially welcomed me into this community realized this and started sharing my page on hers. How elated I was I when I had ten people following my page, then 100, then 1,000, then 10,000, and now over 40,000 sparklers, and it is still growing. I could not believe my eyes. There were actually people out there just like me, hurting, feeling unloved, alone, and needing to find a reason to smile each and every day. I had no idea that so many would resonate with what I wrote, with the feelings that I felt each day.

The healing and growth that I have experienced in the last year and a half of being involved in this amazing community of people that comes together to help one another and to make the world more beautiful just makes my heart smile. Now I wake up to a brand new day with love in my heart and a smile on my face. I am prepared to live each day in the moment and to make each one count. I strive to keep my thoughts positive, and I am ready to manifest an amazing future for myself and my family. It really is all about how we think and whether we let our minds take over or whether we decide to follow our hearts, find our passion for life and just let the rest flow. For me, following my heart, living in the moment, and following my passion are what truly make my heart sing. By doing these things, I have changed my world dramatically and have never felt as happy and loved as I do today. Keeping a positive attitude creates a chain reaction of positive thoughts, and the ripples I have seen on my page and others are amazing, to say the least. It truly feels amazing to know that I am a part of something so much bigger, that among all of these pages of uplifting, amazing quotes not just one heart is being healed but that many are being healed. Instead of looking back on their pasts with regret and disappointment, people are starting to look back and see just how far they have come. Now that is truly inspiring.

Each and every day I look forward to bringing forth messages of love and hope, to bring smiles to each and every sparkly, beautiful, gorgeous person who is guided to my page, and maybe, just maybe, bring forth some hope and love that is so very needed by so many. My aim is to let people know that each smile brings hope, hope that tomorrow is a new day and we get to start again. *Smile.* Someone loves you, and that's worth smiling about! And if no one told *you* that they love you today . . . *I do!*

 Rebecca is a mother of two gorgeous little souls and currently resides in New Zealand. She is a a Reiki practitioner as well as the creator and designer of websites to help people market themselves and their businesses worldwide. She has been the driving force behind many regional events in her area as well as marketing campaigns for local and international businesses. She is at her happiest out in nature and spending time with her family, as well as sending out love and smiles on her Facebook page.

http://www.facebook.com/YourInnerSparkle

Chapter 27

Meet Lori Palm and Wes Hamilton
of *Core Passion*

LORI REKOWSKI HAS BEEN an inspiration to us for many years. She has a powerful mission to accomplish with a message to share. And, I believe that Lori wants everyone to know they too have a unique mission with a message to share. As you now realize, she found Facebook to be the perfect gathering place to meet, connect to new friends, and share stories about who they are and what they do.

We were excited when Lori invited Lori Palm and me to share our stories and mission with you and be part of this awesome movement to awaken everyone to their greatness. We're very excited to connect with others on a similar path through Facebook. We'd like to share our stories of healing with each of you so that you can be inspired to see that no matter where you are in life, you too may be inspired to find your path to personal freedom and empowerment.

My story of knowing who I am started when I was 7 years old I felt very connected to something greater than myself. My life was fun, experiential, and exciting until I felt like a victim in 1980 when I was hit by a sand truck on my way to work and "died" for thirty-five minutes. At that time my career was at a peak and then it crashed while I healed for six months. In 1992 I was again at a new peak in my career when the financial market crashed and I filed for bankruptcy, owing millions of dollars. In 1993 I started on a new path to reconnect that greater part of myself. I attended many self-awareness seminars; the practices that touched my soul and spoke to me prompted me to become trained as a teacher/counselor/healer. I became an expert in three ancient modalities, meditation, numerology, and omega-matrix energy work.

In 1998 I met Lori Palm. She was on a similar path to reconnect to her greatness. Here is her story:

The word *secret* has always been a magnet. It draws us into its magic. If someone has a secret we want to know what it is. Sometimes we go to extreme measures to find the secret. The dictionary says that something that is secret is kept from knowledge or view, a secret works with hidden aims or methods; it is designed to elude observation or detection. A secret may be something that is revealed only to the initiated.

I discovered the *secrets* of Core Passion® when I went on a vision quest . . . the quest to find *me.* I was searching for something that I couldn't see and I went to extreme measures to find the intangible, the *secret*. I stepped into the unknown, not knowing which way to go. I felt like I was stepping off the edge of a mountain into thin air. I had no idea where I would land or even if I would land. I was absolutely driven to find out who I was and what I was supposed to do.

And so the amazing adventure began. . .

I jumped into the void with faith and one month's rent. At 47 years old, I left a marriage of twenty-five years to live by myself in a one-bedroom apartment. I believed I just needed some time by myself to sort things through. I had to redefine myself. I had never lived in an apartment or lived by myself before. Feeling guilty for leaving, I took very few of my possessions—a dresser, a desk, a few dishes. I even had to borrow a bed. I owned my own business and it wasn't doing very well because of all the stresses in my life so I moved my business out of the office I was sharing and into the dining room of my apartment. It was a large first floor apartment with a sliding glass door out to a tiny patio and it became my place of sanctuary. I didn't have a table or chairs at first, so I set my desk up in the dining room to look out across the living room and out the big window and sliding glass door. This seventies apartment (complete with harvest gold appliances) was surrounded by mature trees and a little pond. Sitting at my desk, all I saw were huge pine trees. I felt safe, as if nestled in a cabin in northern Minnesota. My financial resources were meager. But I will never forget the feeling of total trust, knowing I was doing what I needed to do and knowing I would be okay, knowing I could take of myself.

As I stepped into the *unknown,* a deeper knowing of who I am came first. During those first months, I didn't have a couch or a comfortable chair to curl up in. I'm a pianist and for the first time in my life, I didn't even have my grand piano. I would sit on the floor and meditate and just *be.* For most of my life I have always been busy *doing,* and I realized if I was going to find those lost parts of myself I would have to be quiet and listen to the whispering of my soul and just *be.* Many times just before we come to the crossroads, we fill our lives with busyness so we don't have to listen to that little voice whispering in our ear. When I stopped doing and began listening, my inner voice started to answer those questions I had never been able to voice before.

My inner voice showed me I was a unique, powerful being with important work to do. I felt I was on my spiritual path connecting to my royal spirit but I didn't know where I was going. I did know that as long as I stayed on the path, I'd be okay.

The same questions kept surfacing: Who am I? What am I here to do? Will I meet a life partner? All new and original thought begins with a focused question, which leads to an exploration. Our answers are all around us but if we don't ask the questions, we will never begin to see and hear the answers. Questions can be dangerous; they require tremendous courage to ask because new questions lead to new ways of perceiving. My adventure was beginning. . . . .

This adventure took me to many wonderful places and I met many incredible people. As I traveled I became very aware. I knew that passion was powerful but I didn't know how multifaceted it was. In my search, I discovered there are powerful energy forces that are encoded within us at birth. I call this energy the Core Passion® Codes. Core Passion® energy is what drives me and you to do what we do, what has always driven us. As I followed this thread of Core Passion® energy in my life back to when I was young, I began to understand that these driving forces have always been there. I realized all of the major decisions in my life were really made based on these driving forces. I was either in the gift or the challenge of my Core Passion® codes. As these energy forces drove my life, they were actually guiding me in my personal growth and assisting me to create my destiny.

As I began to understand the meaning of the Core Passion® codes, I discovered the *first of the secrets hidden in the codes . . . Our greatest gift is our greatest challenge. You cannot have the gift without the challenge and you cannot have the challenge without taking ownership of the gift.*

One of my greatest gifts is found in the Core Passion® Code of Partnership, the gift of understanding others. I intuitively know what people want almost before they know. This great gift is a strong driving force that provides a valuable intuitive resource for me when I am in a relationship, either business or personal. It is the gift of creating harmony between people and within environments.

Ultimately this gift becomes one of my greatest challenges. I am always focusing on others. I am so tuned into their needs and desires that I lose the ability to express my needs. I lose *me*.

The vision quest to find *me* came at a time when I was in the great challenge of partnership. When our identity is threatened, it feels like we are dying. The stories about how I saw myself didn't fit anymore, but I didn't have any new ones with which to replace them. I thought of myself as a mom, a wife, a daughter, a business owner. Those words described my relationship with others in my life but who was I, not defined by anyone else? I had become what I thought everyone wanted me to be and in the process, I lost me. I realized I had submerged so many parts of myself and I had no idea where they were.

Before I could accept the missing parts of myself back, I had to surrender the old beliefs about who I thought I was. Knowing this about myself and understanding the lessons of this Core Passion® Code of Partnership has given me the ability to develop a partnership with myself. Now I am aware when I slip into the challenges of this energy. I take a "time out" to know what I want, and to speak up for myself. This skill has given me the ability to be a really strong intuitive partner with myself and others.

As I developed the partnership with myself, I was also able to have a strong equal partnership with others. I met and married my life partner, Wes Hamilton, in a magical, fantasy wedding in Hawaii. We have an equal energy relationship and, together, we have developed the Core Passion® tools and programs. We believe it is our destiny to bring Core Passion® to the world. Following our passion and purpose, we have created an amazing life.

When you know WHO you are, you know WHAT to do. As I discovered who I am, I embraced my passion and finally said, "I will do whatever I am called to do with whoever comes into my path." I am now a speaker and an author. We work with organizations as well as individuals in the Core Passion® program, using a magical process connecting people with their passion and allowing them to discover who they truly are. The adventure continues . . .

—Lori Palm and Wes Hamilton

 Lori Palm is a modern-day muse, inspiring passion, purpose, and possibilities. An entrepreneur for over forty years, she sees the unseen personal/business opportunities everywhere. Lori guides people and organizations to discover and ignite their passion and develop plans that turn burning desire into gold. Wes Hamilton is a master numerologist, professional mediator, a national teacher of personal growth programs, and a successful real estate broker. Together they created the Core Passion® Assessment and training programs. They use a magical

process connecting people to their passion and creating a space for them to discover who they truly are and what they want.

Find out more at:
https://www.facebook.com/corepassion
www.corepassion.com
https://www.facebook.com/lori.palm
www.weshamilton.com
https://www.facebook.com/Weshamilton
https://www.facebook.com/pages/Awakening-Your-Light-Body

Chapter 28

Meet Cristina Lorga of *Cristina Light*

My name is Cristina Lorga, but on Facebook people know me as Cristina Light. The social circumstances during my upbringing were very difficult. I am originally from Eastern Europe and my family played a major role in the downfall of Communism at the end of eighties in my country, Moldova. We received many threats from the KGB. We were living in a constant state of fear, and the KGB would always try to intimidate us just so that my mother, who was a freedom fighter and a national hero in my country, would basically stop doing what she was doing. Seeing tanks, receiving death threats, and having my parents attacked were very common occurrences. We even had a sniper shooting in the place where we were living. As you can see, my life as a child was pretty scary.

Our family flew to Romania at the beginning of nineties to escape persecution and basically to be safe and not at the risk of losing our lives. My mother had been threatened numerous times that if she did not stop her political activism, her children and her whole family would be killed. There were many attempts by Communists on the lives of my mother, my father, and even my grandmother (who was over 60 then). Numerous people around us, such as family friends, were killed or disappeared mysteriously, and we never heard of them again. One family friend had his face disfigured with acid. Children of some family friends got kidnapped or brutally killed. So words like violence, danger, fear, hatred, death, and anger were very common in my world at that time, and they created very deep wounds in my being which took a very long time to heal and to overcome. I was basically living in terror and fear. I believed that this world was a very unfriendly, cruel place for me from my earliest days. Over the years, I have had to do a lot of work with my inner child in order to overcome this trauma.

I have been interested in metaphysics since I was a child; however, an "official" spiritual awakening happened in the summer of 2008. It was a hard period in my life, and I had hit the bottom and was feeling totally lost. Then one day I heard this voice inside of my head which was not my voice. Well, it was mine; it was the voice of my higher self. That voice told me the following (I will say it first in Romanian because I heard it in Romanian, which is my native language) "Dumnezeu este dragoste, armonie si pace" which means "God is love, harmony, and peace." That was a turning point in my life because I realized that in order to experience love, harmony, and peace all I had to do was to develop an intimate relationship with God. The most intimate relationship that we can ever experience is the one with God, and any external dependence is actually a longing for the internal connection with God. Who has God needs no one and nothing else. Who has God is *whole*. Since I was not experiencing any of that at the time, obviously I turned to God. I decided to turn inward and start my self-healing journey. I decided to reach for the Kingdom of God *within*. Since then meditation has been the most important technique for my spiritual evolution.

After I acquired a lot of self-help tools (such as healing of the emotional body, the mental body, healing of the inner child, and so on), I realized that these tools could help so many other people who had gone through difficult experiences. So I decided to share these tools with others so that they would also feel inspired to leave their pasts behind. Many people have gone through *so much,* and some of them feel really stuck and feel there is no way out. My job is to tell them that there is *always* a way out. Victimhood is so disempowering! Wearing one's wounds as a badge of honor will not take one anywhere!

I post very inspirational quotes written by wonderful authors and inspirational speakers who have changed my life. I also love publishing my own work and in the future I plan to publish a book with messages that come from my own soul. I tell people how wonderful they are. I encourage them to reach to the light within themselves and become emotionally independent, self-sufficient, *whole,* balanced, in tune with their divine selves. I want them to know that very powerful souls choose very difficult missions by incarnating into difficult circumstances and that they are strong enough to overcome anything. The light within them is so needed, and that is why they chose their particular experiences—to share their beautiful light, to learn, to grow. Too many people choose to cling to the suffering instead of learning to let go of it. I advise people to move on and open themselves to the world of infinite possibilities. I believe that the only limitations are the ones imposed by our minds, so I encourage them to dream *big,* because if they can dream it, they surely can live it. All they have to do is to get out of their own way.

We all have *so much* to offer and have so much integrity and beauty, and once we are able to overcome our personal dramas we can build a better life for ourselves and the people around us. Each one of us is unique and has a unique set of skills which no one else on Earth has. The presence of each one of us here on Earth is *essential.* We are all part of the divine plan. The more in tune we are with our divine selves, the more we will know exactly which is our role here at this time. My mission is to offer people the tools to get in tune with their divine selves. We are truly divine beings of love and light. When we are connected with our divine essence, we *are* love, we *are* harmony, and we *are* peace. We remain centered and calm in the midst of the craziest external storms because we draw our powers from within. The less intimate people are with God, the more unhappy they get and the more dependent they become on external things or people, and the more they look for external things to fill up the empty holes within them.

I always tell people that I am not a guru and that I do not want to be looked up to. Going to the Kingdom of God within is a very personal journey. We come alone and we leave this Earth plane alone. Listening to our *own* inner guidance is *so important*! Giving power away to another one is unhealthy. I always make sure that I tell my Facebook friends how magnificent they truly are and that the key for their empowerment lies in both their ability to love themselves and to go within instead of looking for an external source of fulfillment.

My healing journey continues, and I still have ups and downs at times. I am not a guru. I am still in a human body, and I honor my emotions by crying when I feel like crying or laughing when I feel like laughing. I just do not get sucked into the external drama that much. My inner world is so much more interesting to watch and experience than what is going on on the outside. Love is the greatest healer. So whatever comes up in my experience, I send unconditional love to it and I accept it as it is. God sees *everything* with the eyes of love. God never judges, compares, or measures. God just loves because God is love. The more love I allow in my life, the more I connect with God within.

This human journey on Earth is all about learning to express our divine magnificent selves. Deep down within we are all unconditional love, and learning to love in this world despite our traumas, hard childhoods, and so on is what this life is all about. The more love we allow in our lives, the more we return to our natural state. Our divine selves cannot ever be damaged and when we connect to our divine loving essence, we are able to face any challenge with courage and love. One of the most important parts of my mission is to show people how to love themselves because one cannot truly be open to God when one is not able to love oneself.

Namaste and many blessings *always*!

 I was born in the Republic of Moldova in 1981. At the age of 11, because of political tensions during the fall of URSS, my family and I moved to Romania. I started my intensive artistic training at the most prestigious art school in Bucharest, Nicolae Tonitza, one year after I arrived in Romania. Since then, I have diligently pursued various art techniques, such as figure drawing, printmaking, still life, painting, composition, sculpting, book illustration, and so on. In Romania I created mostly representational art that was very anguished and expressionist in nature. I was still very vulnerable back then because of the traumas I went through as a child.

I received my bachelor's degree in engraving and drawing from the National University of Art in Bucharest, Nicolae Grigorescu.

In 2006 I won a two-year full-study fellowship at the University of Iowa in the United States. While getting my two master's degrees at the University of Iowa, I started focusing more on abstract art. This was the time when I experienced a major inner shift (I call it an awakening), and when I made the decision to change myself and not be a slave of my past anymore. I believe that we change the world by changing ourselves first. It doesn't go the other way around; the change *has to happen* from within. Abstractionism was a very fascinating arena for me to explore because it is very connected to the subconscious mind. Since I graduated from the University of Iowa, I have returned to representational art.

https://www.facebook.com/cristina.light1
https://www.facebook.com/pages/Cristina-Lights-archive-of-Enlightened-quotes

Chapter 29

Meet Agape Satori of *Truebook.org*

I HAVE ACQUIRED VARIOUS experiences, both professional and personal, in the fields of human resources management, psychology, marketing, counseling, consulting, music composition, and spirituality.

I was brought up in a Christian family but left organized religion in 2005 on my awakening to the global manipulation of human consciousness. Since then I have gone through researching the basics of quantum physics, deeper aspects of Consciousness, advanced information regarding ancient civilizations, in-depth evaluation of conspiracy theories, and lately, something that I call transcendent spirituality with practical realistic implications in the everyday world.

My interest in the "alternative view of things" was born out of my fascination with the universe. Before I even went to elementary school I was already flipping through pages of the encyclopedia, reading about distant stars and galaxies, cutting out pictures of known planetary bodies that I would later use for my first artistic collages. This hobby of mine carried me through my childhood where I was beginning to explore the paranormal world of UFOs, psychic abilities, and ancient history.

Being raised in a Christian family that was very heavily involved with missionary work was not easy but interesting nevertheless. Thanks to my upbringing I have been introduced to many moral values I would otherwise not been taught about in this world we are living in. My big thanks go out to my family who have always been there for me, despite the differences in our perceptions of life as a whole.

After spending many years in the church, having experienced many denominations, having met many genuine and many false figures, and having done years of "peeking" into the alternative View of the world, I decided organized religion is just not the right type of coffee for me. Suddenly I was immersed in the world of conspiracy theories that kept me busy for at least four years in a very thrilled and rigorous way. I have never been the type of person to support sensationalist claims and attention-seeking behavior, so it was hard to sift through all the information available.

My journey took me through being angry at the powers that be via information shared by Alex Jones, which only dragged me down into despair and depression, to slowly letting go of my long-term indoctrinated fear of being "thrown down to the pit of sorrow" by the Christian God, thanks to people like David Icke who connect the world of conspiracy theories to nonreligious spirituality.

After doing this very extensive research for about five years, I decided to take what I learned and give it to others, sharing my knowledge of the physical and the metaphysical through my art in audiovisual production and my Facebook page.

The main reason I started serving others was to eventually create a place in the virtual world, such as Facebook, where *all* information from the areas of science, spirituality, technology, health, history, and others will be available for everyone. Also, projects that focus on creating change in the world will have the opportunity to present themselves and get connected with the right kind of audience. There have been many attempts to create a project of this sort, but most of them have not been able to deliver a high-level professional approach, which is necessary when one desires to make a positive global impact.

I have been working on this massive initiative for two years now and we are very close to completing a high-standard, professionally created portal.

My aim for the future, after the completion of my current vision, is to use this portal in the virtual world to allow me to help in the co-creation of a visible physical change in this world. I am being requested more and more to present my knowledge at lectures, magazines, and radio shows across Europe, and I hope that one day, I will be bringing education, inspiration, and empowerment to all places on our beautiful planet Earth.

 A background in Human Resource Management, Agape has worked for major 4 star hotels in Europe recruiting and staffing high profile employees to manager positions. With an education in Personal Psychology, he's beginning study in Neuro-linguistics and Transpersonal Psychology next year. He is now running a business company in finance, including working on a project in Zambia (where his partner received10 million USD to change a hunting reserve into animal protection reserve.) Agape is also working on a project focused on Rainforest protection in South America and Asia.

One of his greatest passions is in producing music and videos, which share inspirational and educational message in a modern technological format.

https://www.facebook.com/Truebook.org
www.AgapeSatori.org
http://www.youtube.com/playlist?list=PL595E97B4800A1F90
Rain Forest Protection http://www.raintrust.com/

Chapter 30

Meet Jennifer Hough of *The Vital You*

The Wide Awakening of the
Heaven-on-Earth Construction Crew

I'M NORMAL, REALLY I am. Or at least that's what I kept trying to prove to myself and those around me for the first few decades of my life, until I realized something . . . I love the "not belonging club." Not rebelliously, outspokenly, or pushily though. I didn't always love it either. I felt for most of my life that I didn't belong, or that there were parts of me that were misunderstood, and as a result I resigned to living aspects of my life beating my own drum. After all, what kind of guy would like someone who doesn't fit in, what kind of jobs could I get when I was always creating new ways to do stuff, and how would my teachers like dealing with me when I questioned everything that didn't make sense in my mind about science, religion, and work? I did resign to beating my own drum, however, as though that way of living was the "booby prize," and the people that chose to go along with everyone else were having the real lives.

Then something (actually a few things) happened.

There were a few events in my life that stand out as catalysts. Before being in the beautiful marriage of the hearts relationship that I am in now, I went through some life-altering experiences when I divorced a man that I love because my life was calling me forward. It didn't make sense, but I knew I had to leave, and I followed my heart. It took courage. More important, it showed me that it takes courage to follow your heart, that it's worth it (an understatement) and that following your heart is rarely rational. Most of all, I realized that I was being guided from somewhere that felt true and right. Since then I've spent my life not only communing with my higher guidance, but assisting others to find mastery by integrating with that very guidance. It has been so fulfilling to teach others the skills to hear with clarity and have the courage to follow that same guidance.

I also worked corporately for years, and the transition to what I do now has been formative. It's a pretty big leap to go from accounting and economics to seeing into other dimensions and activating subatomic DNA, if you know what I mean! My life in the corporate world was essential to assisting me to create my current business's infrastructure. However, like everything that I have done, I did not listen to the books or the corporate world when formulating my business. I actually worked with consciousness to create a business model that breaks the rules of competition and making money. We don't operate from a model; we actually fit the model to how humanity is shifting on a weekly basis. If we did have a model, it would be called "service and contribution." It is not about our financial gain (although of course we love that as it enables us to assist more people, and we do); it is actually about serving humanity and awakening the masses to the best degree we can in the moment. Every one of our staff is a coach. Every member of the staff is in the moment. In fact, surrendering to the levels of life that we cannot see is the secret to truly flying at the Wide Awakening.

But I am ahead of myself, because before my corporate life and my marriage I had an experience with a particular street kid named Angel that I want to share; our fifteen-minute walk to the psychiatric ward changed my life.

Understand, I came from a middle-class upbringing with parents who cared a great deal for my sisters and me. It was normally dysfunctional. I had no experience with anything else, and, as far as I knew, everyone had a similar life to mine, give or take. Then I started working with street youth at a hostel in downtown Toronto in my late twenties. The contrast of the stories of the street kids I used to work with compared with my upbringing altered the way I saw the world. For two years I worked with transvestites who were disowned, children of alcoholics who were now alcoholic themselves, female and male prostitutes from all walks of life; and I got to know many of them on a first-name basis. I struggled with not inviting them home and I worked more after hours out of inspiration; it seemed I could not help myself. I contributed as much of myself to the job as I could while I was on the youth hostel's outreach van. I lived in the area as well and saw many of them on the street on my way home.

After six months of volunteering, I became a paid youth worker, working in the shelter itself. This was powerful. I wish I could share more stories of inspiration with you, as there were many. These kids were pretty hardened and I suspect that most of the inspirational transformations likely happened when those youth were many years older. There was, however, one young woman who stood out for me. I don't remember her real name but she called herself Angel. I remember her spirit, and our less than twenty-minute relationship changed my life.

My manager was a powerfully spiritual man, now that I look back. He was a shaman to his core. He was probably my first exposure to "crunchy granola" people, as I liked to call them. I was asked by the manager to escort a girl to a different building. She was a beautiful blonde girl with an energy that glowed across the room. She weighed about ninety pounds! She called herself Angel (many of the girls changed their first name to Angel, perhaps in hopes of feeling more loved by God or in hopes of opening their lives to just a little more heaven). Normally a much more experienced person would have walked this young girl to the psychiatric ward but they were all busy and I guess my manager figured I could handle it. It was clear Angel had serious psychiatric issues (schizophrenia was the initial diagnosis) and she was on the streets for the first time, extremely vulnerable and not very street smart. She had likely already been approached by drug dealers or introduced to the prostitute trade somehow. Given that I too had not been very street smart, I could relate to her vulnerability. So we walked and I asked her questions about her life and family. She had no filters; her communication was clear and coherent. She told me more than most street kids would have in a year (if they were telling the truth, that is). I held her hand, even though it was against the shelter's rules; I didn't care. She shared about the abuse, the drugs, and the pain. What her father and her brother had done to her for years. She cried. I felt it. It was the first time I had been with a "fresh" young person who wasn't yet jaded by survival in the streets. I saw myself passionate and desperate to say something that would show her that she could be okay, that the acts of others had nothing to do with her goodness. I naively attempted to "change her life," show her what was possible, and that she was loved by Creation. I just wanted to hold her. That was definitely against the rules.

The walk was over in eighteen minutes, but the experience lingered within me for days after. When I left her at the psychiatric ward and walked down the stairs I sank to my knees crying, which then turned into sobbing convulsions from the core of my cells. It was like someone showed me that my sister was being raped and I never knew it. Then I was shown the global suffering (by whom or what I didn't know at the time), and it was more than I could take. So many feelings ran through me—guilt, sorrow, confusion about my humanity, anger at her parents, anger at society, frustration that I felt so powerless. Questions raged through my mind. I'd been at the youth hostel for a year. Why did this affect me so much? Should I have taken her home? Was I arrogant even to think I could help? Did some souls come to the planet to suffer? Should I surrender to the "way it is" and just do the best I can? You see, in youth work, so many of the counselors get burned out or numbed, sort of like a doctor who sees a lot of hurt and death. That doesn't have to happen, but it does. It certainly would have been the least painful route, and I understand now why one might choose to numb out.

It was a choice point in my life. Should I acquiesce and simply deal with it, become cynical and try to forget and move on? Could I add somehow to the good in the world and actually do something that would make a difference? I know, I know, I'd been told by my father earlier in my life that I was too Pollyanna, and had rainbows coming out my backside! This was one of those times in my life where all of the dreaming that world peace and inner peace was possible came right to the forefront. It was a crossroads that I didn't recognize at the time. I chose to be the change in the world, live out my piece of the puzzle of expanding heaven on Earth and assist others to do the same. I would not stand by when I could participate in the co-creation of a world where each soul could be free, peaceful, and fulfilled.

That event caused clarity within me about my contribution in this world, that I could do something that would make a difference in a way that shifts paradigms so powerfully that there would no longer be room for people to forget their magnificence, and that others could do that too. Parents and children would have the capacity to follow their hearts' callings, regardless of circumstances, because we are all children of Creation, not children of biology.

This perspective gave me the capacity to still see street kids and tragedies in the world, without having their stories take me out at the knees. These experiences catalyzed my passion, and my knowing that the awakening of humanity was inevitable. I was going to fully participate in my piece of the puzzle of expanding heaven on Earth.

Pollyanna it is. Bring it on, life.

Over the past twenty years working with others that feel a sense of urgency to fly forward by listening to their own internal callings, I have felt a shift. There is a distinct cultural awakening occurring that includes following that cosmic guiding voice. Humanity now seems to be poking its head above the density, and seeing that there is more to life, from what I have witnessed in the programs I teach. More and more people are coming forth to say that they have felt the same "on the outside-ness, and doing their own thing-." What if we've all been in training to lead the way out of "fitting in" so that we can all "fit out." Maybe as we each have more courage to follow our hearts, it is creating a world where all are getting to be free. The not-belonging club (regardless of how perceptively big or small a role we are playing) is comprised of way-makers. The irony is, most not-belonging club members don't even want to belong! Don't worry, it's not really a club; it's more of an expanding consciousness.

Now I live my life assisting those who feel that what is available in life is "something more." I commune directly with consciousness and the collective guidance levels of those I work with and humanity. I am a crunchy granola. I assist others to embody the skills, courage and yes-ness that have served me so magnificently. I mean what's the fun of this journey if we cannot pay it forward? The more people there are who feel free to play, dance, and create, the more people we get to co-create with and the fewer Angels have to walk the streets. At least that's how I feel about it. Don't get me wrong, I'm still blossoming and expand-ing forward with myself as well. Nothing in my life stands still for long, because I experience creating as expanding enjoyment, and who doesn't want more of that?

I remember recently standing in Peru, in front of one of the trip par-ticipants and each of us touched one another just above the mid point of our eyebrows and looked into one another's eyes (our third eyes). We saw past the veils of protection in a way that was so profound, we both wept. It was a return to innocence. I could feel my higher levels calling me to "see her," as in the movie *Avatar,* and beyond. What I saw was so much beauty, all of her etheric bodies, all of the guides that were assist-ing her, and angels around her body. I had seen this many times before, but this time was different. It was clear to me that she was not an excep-tion and in an instant I saw all of this around each of the participants. I was ecstatic. And the woman whom I was standing with instantly opened, and to this day her life is in a flow of love and abundance that is indescribable. That is what is available for all people—no exceptions.

I am blessed to live this life; however, I am even more blessed to be able to assist others to find congruence with who they are, their flow, their piece of the puzzle of heaven on Earth. We can change the world, and we do.

By the way, as it would happen the universe has seen fit in the past few months for me to meet several people in our programs who were just like Angel, living on the streets. The question I get asked most is if I ever met her again and find out what happened. I don't think I've ever met Angel herself, but many other angels that told me that there was someone who loved them enough when they lived on the streets, that the imprint of that love stayed with them. It was that imprint that assisted them to remember their beauty and magnificence. Every thing you do and every act you make affects someone somewhere. It's time to awaken.

Jennifer Hough is a Seer, Alchemist and Best Selling Author. Her work is to assist each of us to awaken to our innate abilities beyond the 5 senses, to live life in flow and passion, and to truly experience our lives as "a piece of the puzzle of Heaven on Earth" in this lifetime. Her magnetic style and authenticity have blown audiences away all over the world. She's been emanating her special kind of light from Peru to Hawaii to Toronto to Germany and Australia..........igniting flames of peace, passion and effortless flow where ever she goes. Jennifer is a supreme lover of life that will activate your cellular YES, making that little voice in your head highly uninteresting to listen to. Her mission is to cause Heaven within so we can all bring Heaven with us where ever we go! The programs she teaches are: Get Out of Your Own Way™, The Personal Mastery of Awakening and The Awakening Coach Training Program. She also takes those ready to have the full experience on Awakening Adventures all over the world. A sample of where Jennifer's Journey has led her to speak:

- The Holistic World Expo, 2007 to present – Toronto, Canada

- The Millionaire Women's Bootcamp, 2009 to present – London, England

- The Master's Gathering, 2009 to present – Global

- Dialogues of the Heart with don Miguel Ruiz and Dan Gutierrez, 2010 - Global

- Journey's for Conscious Living 11/11/11 Conference – Denver, Colorado

- The World United Conference 12/12/11 – Hyderbad, India

- Power, Passion & Profits, 2011 & 2012 – Phoenix, Arizona

- Peru, Costa Rica, Ireland, Mexico, Australia and growing . . . .

- CORPORATE: IBM, Procter & Gamble, Criterion Research, The Royal Bank of Canada, Grand & Toy, Ontario Government

Jennifer's Books:

Co-Author in Best-Sellers:
Millionaire Woman, Millionaire You –
A Life of Purpose, Wake Up, and Live the Life You Love

Author:
The Ultimate Holistic Cookbook & The School of Unlimited Life

Jennifer's been in the following movies:

What is Possible?
Transformation
And continues to work on her film *The Mission Possible* about children creating projects of great change and going far beyond our perceived limits, assisting us all to awaken

Television and Radio appearances:

Small Business, Big Ideas
The Wide Awakening
SOUL Radio
https://www.facebook.com/thelawofawakening
http://www.thevitalyou.com
http://www.jenniferhough.com
http://www.thepractitionermentor.com
http://www.thewideawakening.com
http://www.blogtalkradio.com/SoulRadio

Chapter 31

Meet Heather Richardson of *Alice in Wonderland Teatray*

I RUN ALICE IN Wonderland's Teatray and I also briefly ran a page called Standing Up to Corporate Power; there's a story in there!

I do not believe that I am defined by my life events, but that I define myself by my legacy—the impact I have left on the places I have been to and the people I am in contact with. But life experience, if not a definer, is certainly a shaper, and I am shaped today first and foremost by the fact that I am an alcoholic in recovery. After many years battling to fix my obsession to drink and change the way I felt I finally gained enough humility to accept the only solution I have found that works, a spiritual twelve-step program way of living. And boy, does it work!! But to reach that level of humility, to accept that I didn't know what I was doing and needed to help myself (not wait to be rescued), I had to lose everything. I had to lose the ability to work; I was on the brink of losing my home;

I had lost myself, and, worst of all, I lost custody of my two beautiful and amazing children. I cared so little for myself it was inconceivable that anyone cared for me, and I had no comprehension of the damage I was doing to my family, kids, ex-husband, and parents because I was consumed by fear and self-loathing. The fact that these people loved me, begged me to sort myself out, it meant nothing. And then one day, I woke up. I found a strength that was not my own, the obsession to drink and harm myself left me immediately. I got a program, and, miraculously, my children came back to me just six weeks into my recovery. I'm now nearly three years clean and sober.

During this time I worked tirelessly to help others like me. Professionally, I have been a management consultant for most of my life, paid to advise others on conflict and problem resolution, to lead, to communicate and articulate complex messages simply. I transferred this into working with other alcoholics. I loved helping others! And I was good at it! Things were great at home And then I fell in love, and fell prey to a predator, a man I now know leaves behind a trail of unwanted children and heartbroken women. But for me, and my children, it was real! And we were in a dream world, where I had a new life partner, my children had a 24/7 man in the home, and we planned a new baby. And then, as abruptly as this whirlwind started, less than ten months later, I was left, with an engagement ring, a very early pregnancy, a broken heart, and two distraught children. It got worse, much worse, and I will not put into print the details of those hellish months, but my home was broken into, my children terrorized, my baby lost, and my character assassinated to somehow prove I deserved such treatment. I was diagnosed with PTSD and I had days where I would be shaking, wracked with grief and guilt and fear, and unable to move; I would "chin" my phone to one of a handful of amazing friends I had, and whisper, "I can't move. Please help me with the children." I did not drink nor take prescription drugs during this time—not because I'm a martyr, as the drugs certainly would have helped, but because as I stated at the start, I am shaped by many things, addiction being one. It was too risky even to try drinking or drugs. During this time, I had faith that while I had *no way* of understanding why this was happening, when for two years I'd done nothing but help others, that I *would* learn. So I learned. I learned that I can love, properly, which is why my heart was broken. I learned what true friends are, I learned compassion from them, I learned to be careful, I learned that envy is such a deep-rooted issue in our world that, if you are happy and doing good, there are many waiting for you to weaken and knock you down. It was this envy that got me and Facebook together. I felt I'd lost my voice during all of this, I felt that I was in a glass screaming and everyone could see me but could only hear noise and not what I was saying; I felt like the woman who is raped by the town hero: He knew, she knew, but everyone else just didn't believe that such awful things could be true, so she was dismissed as a fantasist, or someone who somehow "brought it on herself by wearing a short skirt." It was appalling. And I needed to shout. And there was Facebook. So I shouted.

And I got through it. I believe in God, but not a labeled description, just a resource that is there for me, a relationship that is personal to me; a lookout, a guide, my intuition, my strength, and my courage. And God gave me glimpses of being okay: a laugh or a smile from the children, a trip to the park with a friend. And bit by bit those glimpses got closer together and then I was happy again! Happier than when I'd first found a spiritual way of living, because not only did I have that, I also had depth.

I was pretty much blogging on Facebook, making a lot of people laugh as I started to laugh again myself, and I also started to make my own posters, serious and not. A friend said I should think about starting a page. So I did. I suspected that I could help others again, this time not just addicts or alcoholics, but anyone suffering; however, I didn't know what would happen. Not many of my friends liked my page! I expect they were grateful I'd stopped filling up their news feeds! Although I have to say a lot do now. I wasn't ever disheartened; I make the posters and write because I love to. but then another page saw me and contacted me. He opened the doors to other pages and before I knew it Alice in Wonderland's Teatray was growing fast. And today I know from the comments that I get that I really do help. This is a priceless gift.

Alice has been great for me! It has been the end of my healing, a continued life healing, and the start of a new period of growth. I've learned new skills as a photographer, I have tapped into this artistic and creative side of me I had suspected but wasn't familiar with! I paint, I write, I draw, and I love it.

And then the rather odd little story of the second page. In a rather bizarre twist, it was this page, the one that I only ran for a few weeks that led Lori (the creator of this book) and me to meet. She spotted a poster I had made, which said "I told this company that Facebook gave me a voice, they scoffed, but it does and I'm not afraid to use it," and she contacted me. I had moved recently, and encountered real problems setting up the house with Wi-Fi, TV, phone services, and so on, as I live in a very small town in the middle of nowhere. I waited weeks for the service to be installed (it cost me a fortune in mobile Wi-Fi to keep Alice running), and then it wasn't what I'd asked for, been offered, or expected. You would think that as this service came from the largest U.K. telecoms provider and owner of all the lines, it would be a simple complaint and rectification. It was not, I was intimidated on the phone, I was told it was "impossible to complain" about that company's services, that I was tied into a contract whether I liked it or not, and, unfortunately, because of the installation delay my "cooling-off" period to change my services had expired before I even knew what I was getting! No, I believe in love, compassion, kindness *strongly*! But I also *strongly* believe in justice. At the point I was told it was "impossible to complain," I was incredulous. If I, a capable independent woman who lives a pretty Zen existence, was reduced to bouts of tears and angry frustration in the many hours of phone calls this process involved, what about someone old, frail, young, or inexperienced? I don't believe in right or wrong; I believe in just and unjust. What I was experiencing was outrageous. The company wanted a small fortune for me to exit the contract, this despite my services being unusable. And because of the attitude I knew I would not be alone. But people are too scared to stand up; it is easier just to accept. So I started a new page, called Standing Up to Corporate Power. And it worked. I did receive an apology from the company, the services I did not want were retracted without fee, and I was offered a continued discount on the services I wanted to keep. At one stage they said to me "we are not going to treat you any differently just because you run a Facebook page."

I replied, "I do not expect you to treat me any differently. I expect you treat all your customers a damn sight better."

I did not want to end the page just because I got what I wanted, but at the moment I do not have time to run both. The simply beautiful words I have had from Alice's fans have made clear to me where the value lies. Currently, I am writing a children's story and a novel, as well as producing posters into other forms not for Alice. As all the images and words are original, people have started to ask me where they could buy them! At the time of going to press you still can't very easily, but I'm working on it! Alice has to and will always be my priority. Yet two miraculous things happened from this second page, first, that Lori and I found each other, and second, that I have direct experience of using Facebook as a social medium tool for change. And if I can, so can you.

 Heather Richardson is a writer, artist, and freelance change consultant from England. She lives with her children and a dog in a small picturesque town nestled in the South Downs. She finds it quite amusing that having traveled and lived all over the world that now, at the fun age of 40, she has happily chosen to settle not far from where she grew up. Heather is possessed of a typically British and daft sense of humor, hence Alice in Wonderland's Teatray; it's the name she gave to her iPad, as it is "both flat and magical" and where she does most of her work.

https://www.facebook.com/WonderlandsTeatray

Chapter 32

Meet Michael Perlin of *3 Magic Words*

EVERY FILMMAKER HAS THEIR story, that they went against all odds and made the impossible happen and cut corners each step of the way with obstacles in their path. But my story is how I made something out of nothing. All I had was an idea, a dream, and I had no idea how I was going to manifest it into reality. In 1992, I was living in Dallas, Texas, fresh out of college with an economics degree. I was waiting tables at Macaroni Grill. My metaphysical interests kept me busy. I read everything I could find, Neale Donald Walsch, *Illusions, The Four Agreements, Celestine Prophecy,* Carlos Casteneda, Manly P. Hall, Edgar Cayce, and many more. I listened to audiotapes on cassette, practiced meditation, yoga, and learned everything I could about the spiritual side of life.

The world that I lived in just didn't seem right to me. We were still fighting wars over land, race, and religion. Nobody seemed to care that this was still going on. It was like people just accepted it the way it was and wanted to stay oblivious to what was happening on our planet as a whole. But I never accepted it as the reality that I was going to live in, and I set out to change it. I started to see a pattern—that there was actually a solution to the problem. There were so many spiritual ideas and teachings out there that seemed to be saying the same things about non-violence and love but in so many diverse ways. I saw this as part of the problem. So I decided that if I found a common spiritual theme, I would repackage it into a language for the common man and try to bring it to the world by the year 2012. When I started researching into metaphysics in the early nineties there was no Internet. So I had to physically go to libraries and visit my local used bookstores to find information. I stumbled on an old book called *"Three Magic Words,* by U.S. Andersen, and in it was the answer I was searching for. This became the inspiration to create the movie, and I planned the move to Los Angeles.

I told my dad that I was going to move to Los Angeles and pursue a screenwriting career. He said, "Absolutely not. Do you know how hard it is to make it in Hollywood? Do you know how many people try and fail?" I remembered the fortune cookie I received when I was 10 years old and it changed my life. "One of the great pleasures in life is doing what other people say you can not do." So I went against the odds and without support. I didn't receive a dime from anyone for my travels. I began the road trip with my friend Scott from Texas to California, on bounced checks and a borrowed gas card. We lived out of my car, showered at the beach, and ate 99-cent hamburgers. I luckily landed a temp job serving food for a catering service. That's when I started writing my next screenplay. Max Christensen, whom I'd met previously in Dallas, was the first spiritual teacher who inspired me on my path. So I wrote a screenplay about him, called *The Master.* I took a job at a metaphysical bookshop in Venice, where I absorbed everything you can imagine on mysticism and metaphysics. I went in and out of odd jobs and finally went back to school for editing, motion graphics, and filmmaking at Santa Monica Community College, while working full-time at a film school.

I had this idea, this message—a common theme that I knew I had to reveal somehow to the world, but I had no idea how I was going to do it. I put out two more screenplays, an ancient Egyptian time travel piece, and a script called *Atlantis* about a love story set in the backdrop of Ancient Atlantis. I pitched my stuff around for some time but could not sell anything or get an agent because it was "not commercial." I finally landed a job in postproduction and started editing and learning from hands-on experience. That's when I realized that 1997 was a little too early for metaphysical filmmaking. Hollywood didn't want this stuff and no one was willing to help me get my stuff made. So I got credit cards and bought up my own equipment, went to festivals, spiritual gatherings, drum circles, and Indian gurus, and shot whatever I could on my new Sony DV camera. The digital world was changing exponentially by the day, so keeping up with the technology was difficult but I managed to do it. And then high-definition (HD) video finally became a reality. I quickly learned that what used to be a rich man's game, now anyone could do with a prosumer HD camera. I saved every penny I earned, and bought one. I ran into my good friend Maura Hoffman, and told her that I wanted to make a movie with the special message I discovered. She said, "Well, I happen to know some of the people who know that message and I can get them for you!" So, with no money, a little knowledge, and a two-person crew we began the project. I got fired from my job and took a year off to write the screenplay for *3 Magic Words*. While living on unemployment, I searched for the funding to hire a full crew and make the film. A year passed and there was no money. So I decided to take it on alone.

The biggest challenge in making and completing the film was starting out with no money, no support, and no experience (except for the short film "Skeptic" that I had tried to make and that fell through the cracks). So I purchased all my own equipment on credit cards, and borrowed some lights. I threw a green screen up on the wall and with the help of my friend, Maura, I began contacting the individuals who had the most impact in people's lives. People said "No," "You can't do that," "It's impossible," "Give it a rest," and "You need to pursue a real career."

It's comments like these that gave me the fuel to carry on. They actually made me stronger and more determined.

Together, Maura and I brought in the guests for interviews and I prepared all the footage I shot over the years from the many spiritual events I attended and put them all together and began the edit at home with a fifteen-inch Sony Vaio laptop, using Sony Vegas editing software. I had to take an ice pack out of the freezer to set my laptop on so it would stay cool while it rendered the rough cut for three days. The first cut of the film was a disaster. Another year passed and I had to move on to other things. The film was at a dead end. I knew that I had to get someone else on the project or it would never happen. Through a friend of a friend I was referred to a professional director of photography (DP)/editor who was interested in remaking the entire film at a very low cost. He told me he could reshoot it, reedit, and compose the music and score. But money was still a problem. So I approached my family. They are not investors or risk takers and for them, it was not about helping me out but more about a return on investment. So they told me they would consider splitting it if I came up with a business plan.

I spent the next three weeks staying up all night working on a business plan. Grandpa took a look at it and said, "Well, it was very well written but I just don't see how this genre is very commercial." There's that word again, I thought to myself. So, I was back to having nothing and no method of getting the project made. I paid the new DP to put together the trailer that I reedited myself and put it out on the Web. Gudni Gudnason, who was a guest in the film, saw the trailer and generously provided us with the remaining funds that I needed to get the film remade. I found Cameron Smith, our narrator, on Facebook at the last possible minute. The plan was to drive out to Joshua Tree and shoot all his narrations in the mountains in a beautiful setting with trees and sun. It rained out on us and the whole plan faltered. We only had that day to shoot it because of schedules. All hope was almost lost. Cameron mentioned to us that he was the caretaker at the Ox Yoke Retreat Center (part of Yogananda's organization) and that he had the keys to five homes. He suggested since it was raining we could make it a night shoot and shoot in each of the homes. But we did not have any lights. So we went to the new location and brought every lamp we could find into the room, and we had to figure all this out without extension chords. I had to use an old broken teleprompter that went too fast. For the next nine hours I was literally sitting on the floor controlling the speed of the thing by hand to the pace of Cameron's voice as he spoke by the obscure ambient light of antique lamps.

I had to wear practically every hat you can wear in filmmaking since I had little to no money. I tackled editing, animation, titles, graphics, cinematography, sound, color correction, and all aspects of production. This film was made in four years on weekends with a full-time job and a skeletal crew. In November 2010 we traveled to Tokyo and screened the movie with Japanese subtitles. It was a huge success. In April 2010, we had our big Hollywood premiere at the Harmony Gold Theater. We sold out 400 seats the day before the event. On August 22 we screened it in Santa Monica, California, at the Laemmle Monica 4-plex where we sold out three times and had to continue to move into bigger theaters. It looks like Hollywood was finally ready for metaphysics. After finishing the film, I quit my job, sold my furniture, moved out of my apartment and bought an RV to take the film on the road. Homeless and broke, I was able to finish the final director's cut of the film to meet the deliverable requirements on my MacBook Pro at Starbucks, and land a Warner Bros. digital distribution deal.

Now we approach this auspicious date of December 21, 2012 (the end of the Mayan calendar), and the beginning of a new world and a new shift in consciousness for humanity. We have chosen this date to create a cosmic celebration for Earth's entrance into the Golden Age by creating a conscious film experience with the *3 Magic Words* European premiere event in London. At the event, a declaration of consciousness will be announced to the world. World leaders, prime ministers, presidents, and celebrities will sign this document. This is the moment of truth—the day of the final hour when we will all find out if three words really can change the world. I hope they will.

 Michael Perlin is a filmmaker, videographer, editor, writer, producer, director, and effects artist with over a decade of experience in the film industry and his lengthy research into metaphysics, Michael Perlin went against all odds and became the first "Metaphysical Filmmaker" in Hollywood.

He received his B.A. from the University of Texas at Austin before moving to Los Angeles in 1997 to study film and screenwriting. Michael graduated from the Interactive Media program of The Academy of Entertainment Technology at Santa Monica College where he studied video editing, graphic design and motion graphics. He has worked at several post production houses in Hollywood such as Title House Digital, Efilm and THX, as a sound engineer and visual quality technician for many major motion pictures. He was inspired at a young age when he received a fortune cookie that said, "The great pleasure in life is doing what other people say you cannot do." He has a strong connection with the new age community, and has studied metaphysics and world religions for over 20 years.

www.3magicwordsmovie.com
http://www.facebook.com/pages/3-Magic-Words-Movie-Fan-Page-Official

Chapter 33

Meet Dena Patton,
Inspiration and Coaching for Women

Are you working late or are you working yourself to death?

A SUDDEN FEELING OF nausea, shortness of breath, and massive head pain had me leaping from my theater seat and rushing to the restroom. The producer, a good friend, had invited me to sit in on a rehearsal to provide feedback. The outing ended when I suffered a minor stroke—and started a journey that would change my life.

It was 1998. My high-stress lifestyle included running my own marketing and publishing company. I had an office on 57th Street in New York City and a sense of determination that was unstoppable. I was the typical, happy 20-something in New York in the era of *Sex and the City* and Mayor Rudy Giuliani. I was trying to date, get involved in philanthropy, learn about politics, and enjoy the culture. But all of that got sidetracked because I was working myself to death without even knowing it.

I now often ask people, "Are you working late or are you working yourself to death?" You know what I'm talking about: the sixteen-hour days; the desire to please everyone (especially clients) by saying "yes"; the lack of play, joy, and fun; the go-go-go-go-go; and the bad food that fuels it all. I was an entrepreneur, and all of that came with the territory, or so I *thought*.

But I quickly learned that failing to manage my own capacity, boundaries, and health were deadly habits, and I discovered to my surprise that a lot of other female entrepreneurs (and females in general) struggled with the same demons. Years later, I found out that it's often referred to as the Superwoman Syndrome, and research shows that there are horrible consequences to it: addiction, divorce, migraines, heart disease, depression, jail, and even suicide. For me, 1998 was a rough year, but it changed my life and my path forever—and for the better.

I hired a life coach to reprioritize my boundaries, reconnect my body and soul, and redirect my career. Like most women, I lived a busy life and didn't want to slow down my superwoman lifestyle, but the one thing I did know was that I wanted to be a *well-balanced* superwoman instead of an exhausted one. Looking at my clients, associates, and friends, I could see the exhaustion in their faces, their bodies and, most of all, their spirits. I was saddened by the lack of joy in most superwomen. In my mind women were put on this planet to bring it *up* not down, but to do that we have to give up being victim, giving up suffering, giving up overwhelm, giving up "fixing," and instead, step into our grace, our power, our brilliance, and our sisterhood.

During that year of recovery (and discovery), I fell in love with the process and the results of coaching. Almost before I knew it, I sold my business (which has since become a successful global Internet company) and began training as a life and business coach for women. It's the perfect career for me because it combines my love of empowering others with my spiritual calling to make a difference for women, my passion for results, and my years of business experience.

That was twelve years ago, when life and business coaches weren't so popular; in fact, most people didn't know what they were.

Forced to be resourceful, I hired myself to do the marketing, PR, and networking for my new business, since those were my strongest skills. My new boundaries allowed me to set normal, healthy working hours and embark on a career that was all about empowerment, education, and inspiration. I got to enjoy more charity work, New York culture, and all of the people and places of the city. Most of all I dove into the books, tapes, seminars, and churches that restored my faith, my mind, and my direction so that I could serve the world in big ways, without losing *my* way.

I also learned to let go of guilt and anything else that robbed me of joy. I no longer felt tied to my to-do list or a slave to my clients. I stopped saying yes to everyone; instead, in my consultations I interviewed them to see if *they* were a fit for me. I gave up victim, scarcity, and fear for a new currency, love. And it had to start with my loving and honoring myself. Then I could start putting people, clients and activities in my life that I loved, and getting rid of the rest. It was a whole new level of success, certainty, and happiness in all areas of my life. When I say "victim" it often had to do with boundaries, broken boundaries. I allowed clients to call on me at all hours of the day and night. I said yes to ridiculous deadlines that had me working eighteen hours a day. I say yes to projects that required capacity at 125 percent. These are signs of a victim who loses her power to her schedule, to her fears (of what happens if I said no to a client), and to the validation of others. Today, whether I am working with a multimillion dollar celebrity, a large company, or a sole entrepreneur I now come from a place of love—ruthless love–and a total stand for their success. I do my best every time, all the time (and I let go of judgment), which is the key to building a business. Do your best, and don't fake it.

I teach women how to manage their capacity and say no to even the most demanding people. I created my own methodology to help women reclaim their three B's: *basics, boundaries,* and *balance.*

The *basics* are the top three to five most important things in your life—things that provide love, fulfillment, and joy. If you know your basics in priority order, everything else becomes secondary or nonexistent.

With your basics in place, you can live accordingly, which leads to choices, leadership, and time management—the *balance* part of the equation. It starts with a commitment to leave stress behind, and to practice leading a balanced life and making balanced choices. When you make balanced choices that honor your newfound basics, you learn to manage your time with integrity and breathing room, and avoid the running-ragged craziness. You learn to know your limits and manage your capacity better. For example, I don't add anything to my schedule after I hit 85 percent capacity for the week, so I have 15 percent just for fun, creative, and joyful stuff (and breathing).

The third "B" is *boundaries*. Imagine that your basics are the flowers in a garden. Your boundaries are the fence protecting the flowers. Balance is the nurturing water and sun that makes them grow. Your boundaries are the invisible lines that communicate your values and your limits to clients, employees, vendors, family, and friends. With these three B's in your life you will start to build a life that is based on love, and with that *everything* is possible: your wildest dreams, your amazing marriage, your multimillion dollar business, and your fun and adventure.

That stroke was the biggest blessing in my life because it has given me ten years of working in the industry of inspiration through facilitating women's retreats (at fabulous resorts that I love), speaking around the country on stages that I love), and coaching women to achieve their dreams. Those very lessons strengthened my relationship with my mother and also brought me back to Arizona after 9/11. She was a struggling single mother most of her life. She knew how to survive, but implementing boundaries wasn't her specialty. The next seven years we had together were magical. More than anything, we were leading our lives by new rules and new boundaries, and taking joy in it.

I was now married to a great man and eight months pregnant, and Mom was joyfully discovering retirement. I was in heaven; I was working in my calling. In addition to coaching and speaking I was creating projects and programs for women. Three-day retreats, Sisters Program for women's ministries and I co-founded a nonprofit called the Girls Rule Foundation for teen girls.

But a diagnosis of stage 4 pancreatic cancer soon rocked our world. At age 60, my mother was given one to six months to live. We mostly talked about funerals and financials, and what would happen if she didn't make it to meet the baby. But the conversation soon turned away from dying and on to living. How do you live joyfully, knowing you are dying? She became a role model of how to live powerfully and joyfully, and how to die gracefully and peacefully. She was lucky: She lived sixteen months and had time to prepare and say her good-byes (which she did through her own celebration-of-life party that was filled with so much love you could taste it). I was so inspired by her transformation from being a victim of cancer to being in love with her life, that I added a chapter, "Powerfully Living, Gracefully Dying" in my upcoming book. It was a joyful and challenging sixteen months, but I'm thankful that I had enough consciousness to be present to witness it.

But that's not the case when death comes from a heart attack, stroke, suicide, or sudden accident. There's no preparing. So you have to ask yourself: Do I love like I want to? Do I forgive like I want to? Do I use my business to share my spirit, gifts, love, and passion?

I encourage you to know that you are the perfect being God made you to be and your gifts are so very valuable. Every day we have the choice to be an exhausted superwoman, or the well-balanced superwoman. Which will you choose? It's a *daily* choice and sometimes you will not feel like being the loving, well-balanced superwoman. That's okay, but promise me this, that tomorrow you will try again. Don't you know the world is waiting for you to share yourself and your gifts with it?

Below are my top ten tips to help you build the practice of being a well-balanced superwoman:

Honor yourself by setting realistic limits, managing your capacity (85 percent) and saying no often.

Use your business (or projects) as a platform to give your gifts, joy, spirit, and love to the world.

Create a self-care plan, and stick to it. If *you* are unhealthy, your business will be also.

Simplify. Get rid of anything that isn't useful, beautiful, loving, or joyful.

Don't get consumed by your roles (business owner, wife, mother). Step out of that role daily for ten minutes for meditation/prayer along with doing an "inventory check" for life's red flags.

Invest in your future by keeping yourself balanced, healthy, and focused. Stop taking yourself so seriously.

Be your biggest fan, not your enemy.

People won't honor your boundaries if you don't honor them *first*. Then others will follow.

Create more play. It matters.

Surround yourself with people who empower and honor you. Not for your title or role, for you.

Dena Patton is an award-winning life and business coach, speaker, and entrepreneur who works with women worldwide who are changing the world. She is a native of Phoenix, Arizona, and helps double and triple women-owned businesses. Her passion is to encourage, empower, and educate women and girls to be their best selves, and help them build lives and careers they love. She has won nine business awards, been featured in thirty-five media stories, and is a philanthropy leader. Connect with her at:

www.facebook.com/DenaPatton
www.DenaPatton.com

Chapter 34

Meet Rebecca Gross Menashe of *Life Coaching and Organizational Development for Tweens, Teens, and Young Adults*

"STAY *POSITIVE*. STAY *PRESENT*. Stay *strong*. Stay *smiling*." These are my *words* used to sign each of my daily posts on facebook pages. Each word represents my beliefs in taking the powerful steps to journey successfully throughout our day. Training our brain to keep our thoughts positive, in the present, strong, and with a smile can lead one to a more successful and energizing day. This positive energy touching and influencing others has the potential to spread like a speeding train down a track.

Fortunately, I had an incredible role model growing up. As a young child, I observed the many kind and inspiring actions of my humble mother. Many of her actions would at times embarrass me, and I could not understand the need for our involvement in numerous activities. These actions and experiences have left a lasting imprint which today guide me through my life's journey. My passion for a greener and "impact free" society, is one specific interest that mother has inspired.

Before my town had a full recycling program in the 1980s, my mother would volunteer and travel to the local community centers to gather the recyclables. We would work with the janitors of the buildings and load the car up with countless bags of cans and bottles, and deliver them to my home, which had a new recycling program. I remember feeling ashamed and embarrassed as we pulled up and unloaded these countless bags delivered to our curbside. In the late eighties, our side of town had a brand new recycling program, which was not fully accepted or understood in the community. The neighbors were not pleased to see the accumulation of garbage in front of our home, and as a young child I was so ashamed of this act. As a grown adult, with three children of my own, these actions have steered my involvement in a greener society and have fueled my passion for an impact free society.

In addition to my mother's passion for the environment, helping others was *high* priority. When the garbage man, mailman, delivery boy, or other worker arrived at my house, they were immediately greeted with water, or possibly even a sandwich to go. Watching my mother, was like watching a disguised angel. One would never know where you may find her, or what journey you were on mission to accomplish. Whether visiting Ms. Finkelstein, an old Holocaust survivor, or doing her shopping errands, life was always full of helping others in the community.

After graduating from college with a business degree, I decided that inspiring children was more my passion. I continued my education and received my master's degree in education from New York University and began my teaching career at the Ramaz Lower School, a private school on the Upper East Side of New York City. Here I began my teaching career and taught various grades ranging from preschool to the middle-school years. When working with the middle-school children, I shortly realized that this challenging yet impressionable age was my passion. Inspiring struggling students to perform well in school became my obsession, and I shortly took on the role of an advisor for the fifth and seventh grade. Here I worked as a role model and liaison between parent, school, and teacher, helping each student perform the best of his or her abilities. This was most rewarding in my teaching experience.

Where can you find me today? Besides studying my favorite discipline of yoga, my other favorite pastime is to walk down the streets of New York City inspiring others and looking for people to help. I'm proud of my connection and relationships with some of these wonderful homeless people living in my area. It is my passion to give people *hope* and put a *smile* on a face. New York City can be thought of as a fast-paced, cold city, but I have found otherwise. I'm amazed every day by the interaction with my fellow citizens, and how a simple smile, and a hello are able to change the *energy* of a crowded New York City street.

Besides my passion of *street inspiration*, as I have coined my pastime, I started a private practice called Pulling together my education degree and a life-coaching certificate, inspiration from Mitch Mathews (Coach Mindset), and others, it has been my passion to inspire this age group toward a healthy, balanced, educated, and motivated lifestyle. Enabling individuals to pursue their dreams, and giving them tools of empowerment are my goals. Unlike traditional therapy which focuses on the past, my coaching is all about one's present and future. How to find what you need to start creating the life you want while thriving within the life you have *now*. As I sign each post on Facebook, "Stay positive. Stay present. Stay strong. Stay *smiling.*" This is my motto and my message to the world!

Rebecca Menashe is a Certified Professional Life Coach and founder of *Life Coaching and Organizational Development for Tweens, Teens and Young Adults*. Rebecca is passionate about her client's connection with a higher purpose and moving them through indecision and doubt to clarity and creation. Rebecca leads her clients on a path of discovery, identifying one's inner guidance along with carving out pieces of life no longer serving a positive purpose. She guides clients to align their core values by spending time in resonant relationships and activities aiming to achieve vibrant, self-confident, clear and ALIVE feelings! As Rebecca's mantra brightly states, "Stay positive, Stay present, Stay strong, Stay SMILING," Rebecca pushes her clients towards a life of positivity, perseverance, and gratitude.

Prior to becoming a certified life coach, Rebecca graduated from New York University with a Masters in Arts from the School of Education. She also received a Bachelor in Science from Rutgers University School of Business. Rebecca spent 15 years as a teen leader and community teacher at a private school, KJ Ramaz Yeshiva, on the upper east side of Manhattan. Here she taught children ranging from Kindergarten to Eighth grade and served as a guidance counselor for teens in the middle division. Before becoming a certified life coach, Rebecca began a tutoring service called *Motivational and Organizational tutoring*, where she motivated and guided a vast age group of students to accomplish their goals.

Rebecca coins on of her favorite past times as *Street Inspiration*. It is not unusual to find Rebecca on the street corners helping various homeless people around the city she loves, Manhattan, New York. People who are in desperate situations are simply inspirational to her, and she strives to help them find sparks of happiness in their surviving days. Her day is not complete unless she is able to bring hope, a smile, or kind word to another in need. As Rebecca has experienced, NOT until one has reached their greatest adversity will they begin to see their true colors and SHINE! She is currently recording her journey and experiences inspiring others in a self-help book featuring the topic on finding inner happiness and contentment.

Rebecca is also a teen yoga instructor and a lifetime student of the healing arts--including meditation, prayer, visualization, holistic healing & yoga. Rebecca resides in Manhattan, New York, along with her husband and their own two teenagers and six year boy. Rebecca brings her PASSION for growth and self-empowerment into her coaching. "I DARE you to step into your own greatness and bring your brilliance into the world. I know you can do it!"

Rebecca's biggest accomplishment is now her OWN LIFE—balanced, joyful and overflowing with Love, Gratitude, Thankfulness, and the daily magic of LIFE.

www.facebook.com/lifecoachingandorganizationaldevelopment
www.facebook.com/motivationaltutoring
https://www.facebook.com/lifecoachingandorganizationaldevelopment

Chapter 35

Meet Vicki Reece of *Joy of Mom*

TWENTY-ONE YEARS AGO I began a wild journey, one which virtually everyone told me was impossible. After two miscarriages then infertility, I was blessed with my first of three precious children. At that time violent and negative toys and messages were all the rage—and children were being bombarded with them. Although I had no resources, money, experience, or know-how to create products that were good for children, I couldn't sit on the sidelines and complain; I needed to do something about it, something to make a difference. I didn't believe companies with vast resources would make the kind of products that moms wanted and children deserved and needed. With passion, obsessive determination, and a good dose of naivety (enough not to believe the naysayers or realize I couldn't do it!) I put it all on the line (literally) and embarked on a wild and gripping journey to empower children and moms.

I worked at WGN-Radio and left there to write children's books to validate feelings. To put food on our table and keep a roof over our heads, I started a small boutique ad agency out of my basement. I worked from the moment I opened my eyes in the morning until around 10 PM. And from 10 PM until around 2:30 AM I worked on my mission. I ended up conceiving and creating multimedia products for children. Every negative, bullying, and scary story affecting children I heard fortified my need to do this.

I was the sole supporter of our family. My husband left his job to be a stay-at-home dad to support me so I could make my mission a reality.

With each step along my path, I had to make the wisest choices. I truly didn't have the room (or luxury) to make mistakes. And even though that was my reality, and as hard as I tried, I still made plenty.

I believed many people who didn't walk their talk. I'd think how did I fall for that? And lo and behold it happened again. There were so much dishonesty and behind-the-scenes games with business people and it didn't seem to matter what position they were in. From independent folks to those that were in the highest senior positions in some of the largest retailers and media companies. It was surprising how ugly and pervasive this was. One message came through loud and clear: They were not interested in helping or empowering moms and children, even if their corporate slogan said so. I knew I'd need to find another way, another vehicle, a different platform to get my message out, and to get the beautiful message of so many other women and moms who had a mission, a product, a service to share.

Hello, Facebook!

I put my page up and immediately began posting, chatting, and sharing from my heart. All that was important to me, all I truly felt others would be inspired by, and being able to share other fabulous message from Facebook pages that I stumbled on and loved!

Immediately I felt a connection with our friends and the love and support of other beautiful pages. I felt a kindred spirit connection, as if I'd known and liked many of my Facebook friends better and deeper than many real-world friends I've known for decades.

I would literally be doing the happy dance at 2 AM if my page got a new friend. A new soul to touch, connect with, form a friendship and bond. Fast forward a year and 59,000 friends later and I still do the happy dance at 2 AM if I see we got another new friend.

Why am I so passionate about helping others? That's tough to put into words. Ever since I can recall (dating back before kindergarten), I've been intensely passionate about connecting, helping, protecting, and supporting kind people. I think it's in my DNA. Last week I met with a friend from middle school. I had bumped into him about three times over the past thirty years. I always adored him, such a sweet heart and soul. When we last bumped into each other, he told me he came out ten years ago and thanked me for always being so nice to him. We chatted as if no time had passed. We parted with him saying let's have coffee soon and with my schedule, I barely have time to shower (figuratively, of course), I new it would be challenging. Although both our intentions were sincere, when we said yes, I don't think he was expecting to hear from me again, or at least any time soon. I texted him the next week to meet for lunch. I felt excited to get together and have this beautiful connection with our past, before so much of life that's been lived. At lunch he told me that I was on his "bucket list." I was so taken aback. He said I was his only friend in high school and he would never forget my kindness. As much as this meant to him, it meant more to me. Sharing his heart with me touched me deeply. I feel this each and every day— hundreds of times a day—with our Facebook friends. When they thank me for doing what I do, I let them know just how profoundly they are touching me, too.

Vicki Reece, Founder and CEO

When Vicki's children were small, she was so taken aback by the all violent and negative toys and messages marketed to children that she had do something about it. As the sole supporter of her family, this transcended a crazy move, this was a calling. With vision, passion, fearlessness, and just enough blind faith, Vicki put it all on the line (literally) and began a wild and, too often, gripping journey. Vicki's vision and fortitude persevered. She conceived, created, and distributed award-winning software, music, and videos for children. She was championed by a burgeoning community of passionate moms she didn't know but connected with her on the most visceral level. Moms who shared Vicki's vision, and, too, wanted to raise the bar of products and entertainment for children. On the back of purely grassroots and organic momentum, Vicki achieved "#1 Best-Selling Media Product" at Wal-Mart stores and online; Category Leader at major retailers such as Sears, Zany Brainy, Discovery Toys, QVC, Toys "R" Us, and Gateway Computers; and was featured in numerous national TV shows including *The View, CNN, Fox & Friends*; network interviews on: ABC, NBC, CBS, WGN, CLTV; and in over 100 newspaper articles and seventy-five magazine features including *Women's Day, Parenting, Child, Vanity Fair, The Wall Street Journal, London Times, Chicago Tribune, Detroit Free Press, Gannet Newspapers,* and *Los Angeles Times.*

Fast forward twenty extraordinary years. Today, Vicki and her Joy of Mom are the culmination of strength, passion, and purpose. This progressive and evolved community connects women and moms around their innermost passions, interests, and causes. To effect change. To be part of a remarkable movement. To connect, collaborate, share, and to keep on passing it on.

Prior to founding GoodThings Media, Vicki owned and ran a successful boutique advertising agency, with clients including Fannie May/Fannie Farmer Candies, Ameritech, Kraft, and Sunbeam. She was also a senior executive at WGN Radio in Chicago and has always been a passionate activist on empowering women. Vicki holds a Bachelor of Arts in Communications from the University of Illinois.

"We can't take any credit for our talents. It's how we use them that counts."
—Madeleine L'Engle

http://www.facebook.com/joyofmom

Chapter 36

Meet Sharon Lund of *Out of the Darkness Into the Light*

SEXUAL ABUSE, EATING DISORDERS, suicide attempts, destructive relationships, HIV/AIDS, and near-death experiences are all topics made for a movie. Imagine one person not only living through these challenges, but thriving from them because the challenges brought her to self-love, wholeness, forgiveness, and living her life purpose. This is my story.

As a child, from the age of 3 to 12, I was raped by my grandfather. His words haunted me for decades - "If you tell anyone I will kill your mommy."

My second husband, Bill, told me I was ugly, stupid, fat, and that I'd never amount to anything. In his eyes I couldn't do anything right. His verbal and mental abuse led me to become anorexic and suicidal. As I leaned over the tub with a sharp shiny razor against my wrist I said my final prayer, "God please forgive me for what I'm about to do, but I have to end this pain and suffering. If there's anything I need to know before I kill myself, let me know now."

Immediately the entire bathroom filled up with the most beautiful bright, white light that I had ever seen. I felt immense love from this light, which I call God. As it surrounded me, I became calm and at peace. Then I heard, "My child, it's not your time to die. Get yourself into the hospital and when you get out, you'll become a healer, teach around the world, and write books."

None of what I heard made sense to me, but I knew I had received divine guidance from God.

I was admitted to the hospital for anorexia and suicide attempts. While in the hospital, part of my healing was to call my parents and tell them about my years of sexual abuse by my grandfather. Once the words were spoken, and the secret was no longer silent, my heart opened, I felt a deeper connection to my parents, and healing began.

After three months in the hospital, Linda, my mentor, helped me connect with my inner child. Before long I was able to give my inner child the love and protection I so desperately needed. I learned and applied powerful mind-body-spirit healing techniques that began to bring me back into wholeness. I felt a deep connection to God and my spirit guides. When I heard their voices I felt immense love and peace within my entire being. I asked for divine guidance and was shown the way.

Before long I found myself teaching visualization, meditation, stress reduction, and body dialogue to gay men in Hollywood. I came to know and love these men. They filled my heart with laughter, honesty, love, and appreciation for every breath of life. And yet these men that I loved were discriminated against, not only by our society, but by their family members.

In 1986, to my horror, I saw my ex-husband Bill on a special produced by Dan Rather, *AIDS Hits Home,* announcing he was infected with AIDS and had infected his wife, who didn't know he had lived a secret bisexual life style. I called Bill and he denied it was he; but I had heard in meditation that it was indeed Bill, and that I needed to be tested. My test results came back positive for HIV.

The doctor told me that I needed to go on AZT immediately, and if I didn't, I would die within six months. I did muscle testing and asked my body if it wanted me to take AZT. The response I received was a weak "no."

I then went into meditation and asked God/Infinite Spirit if it was for my highest good to take AZT. I heard a loud, "No, do not take AZT."

I called my doctor and informed him of my decision. He suggested I get my final affairs in order. I did as he suggested; I finalized a will, durable power of attorney, and even asked my parents to take care of my beautiful, loving 9-year-old daughter, Jeaneen, when I died. My parents agreed.

Shortly after all my affairs were in order, my heart and spirit were lifted when I heard in meditation: "My child, why have you made your doctor God? Why have you bought into his death sentence? He doesn't know how or when you are going to die."

That was an immediate wake-up call. I had made my doctor God. I had bought into his death sentence. How many people when faced with a life-challenging illness give away their power like I did, and buy into what the doctor says, instead of going within and listening to the truth?

I fired my doctor and interviewed others until I found a wonderful holistic woman doctor who believed in the importance of healing the mind-body-spirit. Instead of becoming a victim to AIDS, I allowed the virus to empower me.

As part of my healing, my doctor suggested I go public with my story to break the silence about women becoming infected. Before long I was interviewed in the news, in the newspapers, on prime-time TV shows, and was later invited to appear on *Oprah*.

The media wanted to make me an "innocent victim" because I was a heterosexual woman and I became infected by my husband. However, my main message was, "It doesn't matter how any man, woman, or child becomes infected. We all deserve the same compassion, love, and understanding."

I dedicated my life to the AIDS community, and my daughter, now 13, also became active in the community. I took it upon myself to start the first woman's HIV/AIDS support group at Sally Fisher's Northern Lights Alternatives, and later at Marianne Williamson's LA Center for Living.

I shared my experiences with students at universities and colleges throughout the United States, sat on the board of directors of AIDS Project Los Angeles and AIDS Medicine and Miracles, made policy decisions at the Ryan White HIV/AIDS Planning Council, and was chosen as one of four women to testify at the Centers for Disease Control, to expand the definition of AIDS to include women's symptoms.

With each passing week my phone would ring, and I knew the moment I picked it up, someone on the other end was calling to tell me that one of my dear gay friends had died from AIDS complications. Men were dying, day after day. There was no end in sight.

I knew I needed to do more. I trained with the Night Light program to go into the homes of these dying men and bring them comfort through words, prayer, silence, holding their hands, feeding them, or being with them as they took their last breath of life. These men brought me blessings and gave me love. They will forever hold a special place in my heart.

As more women became infected, I helped to set up the first women and children's HIV/AIDS clinic in Los Angeles. Within a few years, the phone calls turned to women I knew in the AIDS community who, sometimes along with their children, were dying from complications. Why was everyone around me dying? Why had I survived? Was it because I listened to my body, went into meditation and heard not to take AZT? I started to have survivor's guilt.

After working day in and day out in the AIDS community for years, I was burned out and I was divinely guided to move out of California to the red rocks.

Within a year and a half, I came down with AIDS complications, PCP and then MAI/MAC (Mycobacterium avium complex) —severe diarrhea with fevers over 103 followed by chills as cold as ice. For over a year I was in the hospital more than I was out of it. I weighed 86 pounds. I lost my independence and had to completely rely on someone else to take care of me. I no longer had a quality of life. I was suffering and so was my family.

My doctor called my parents and daughter and told them I probably wouldn't make it through the weekend. Jeaneen slept in bed with me that night. I was too weak to talk; yet telepathically we talked a lot. The love between Jeaneen and me is profound.

The next morning after she had breakfast she said, "Mom I'm going to your house to take a shower, is there anything you want from there?" Somehow, I had the strength to say, "Yes, you, to come back to me."

The moment she left the hospital room, my spirit lifted out of my body and I immediately felt healed, and more alive then ever before. Then two spirit beings came to me and telepathically said that they wanted to show me a review of my life. In each scene they said, "Look at the difference you've made in these people's lives." Then I felt myself go through the tunnel of light and saw gray beings on the outside of the tunnel. It felt like the gray beings wanted to grab a hold of me so that they could get into the tunnel.

Suddenly, the most brilliant, loving, warm, bright light, brighter then we've ever seen here on this Earth plane, came toward me and I became one with the light of God. Telepathically, I heard, "My child, unlike the time before, this time you have a choice. You can remain with me or you can return, but before you make your decision I want to show you one more thing."

Instantly I was reliving, *not* reviewing, but *reliving* being pregnant with my daughter, feeling her kick within my womb, giving birth to my daughter, holding her in my arms and breastfeeding her, and doing various things throughout her eighteen years of life, including our AIDS work together.

Then a spark of light hit me and my spirit was back in the tunnel with the light of God. Telepathically, I was asked, "My child, what is your decision?"

The intense love, healing, and peace I felt in the light of God was so profound. I expressed in sincere love, "I need to return to my daughter."

Immediately and without warning, I was back in the hospital bed. I still looked like a skeleton, but for the next hour or so, I could see bursts of the God light going into every cell of my body, sparkling and vibrating. The healing power of God was restoring me cell by cell. The sensation felt like effervescent bubbles.

When Jeaneen returned, my color was restored, and I had a sparkle in my eye. That afternoon I was able to get out of bed and walk with Jeaneen down the hospital corridor. My doctor considers it a miracle.

Indeed it was a blessing!

Whatever challenges you may face, you can become a victim or allow your challenges to empower you. Know that on the other side of every challenge is a blessing.

I truly feel blessed and honored that my life is now being divinely guided, as I allow God to flow through me with ease and grace. Allow all your challenges to empower you and know that the gift that comes from them can enhance not only your life, but also the lives of other's. We are all connected. We are all one. There is no separation. There is only love. Love and respect yourself, love and respect your fellow man, love and respect all of humanity and all the various kingdoms. Life is precious! You make a difference! You are greatly loved!

Through Facebook, I've been inspired, supported, encouraged, and connected to amazing women and men who are making a profound difference throughout the world. Reach out to friends, new and old on Facebook. Perhaps you'll find the strength and courage you so deeply desire for healing, friendship, love, and oneness.

 Sharon Lund has danced with life and death throughout her life having overcome nine years of sexual abuse as a child, anorexia, suicide attempts, destructive relationship, HIV/AIDS, and two near-death experiences. Sharon is not a victim! She has embraced her challenges, which has seeded the gifts, and wisdom she shares throughout the world.

Sharon's experiences have inspired audiences throughout the United States, Canada, Europe, Russia and Japan. She has appeared on *Oprah, 48 Hours, Eye on America*, CNN and other shows. Sharon was featured in the November 07 issue of "O" the Oprah Magazine and was honored to accept a personal invitation from President Clinton to speak at the White House.

Sharon is the founder of Sacred Life Publishers and Sacred Life Productions. She is the author of the award-winning book *Sacred Living, Sacred Dying: A Guide to Embracing Life and Death, The Integrated Being: Techniques to Heal Your Mind-Body-Spirit* and *There is More . . . 18 Near-Death Experiences*. She is also the co-producer of the award-winning documentary *Dying to LIVE: NDE (Near-Death Experiences)*; and *Mustang Man: How a Wild Horse Tamed a Vietnam Vet.*

Sharon's life is about service to God and humanity, empowering people to be all that they can be, and to embrace the sacredness of life and the Oneness of All.

www.SacredLife.com
www.SharonLund.com
https://www.facebook.com/sharon.lund.73

Conclusion

I'd like to thank you all for taking the time to give yourself the gift of inspiration. Society is hungry for inspiration these days, and the millions of people who are daily subscriber to these Facebook pages are evidence of that. As you have read, some of our authors have awakened to their true power or core essence, whatever you wish to label it, by instantaneous "a-ha" moments; some through tragic accidents; and others gradually by a series of events showing up in their lives that assisted them in owning their power and stepping up to the plate to be of service with their passions. They knew that something *had* to change in order for them to find contentment, peace, and overall wellness in their lives. And, change it did. I hope that we've inspired you to make the changes necessary for you to discover your core passion and purpose.

I must say, that the biggest signpost that many of us experience when a big change in our lives needs to occur, is when we experience anger or rage at a situation, person, or event. We get a sense of powerlessness from the experience and often feel like we have no control, which fuels our anger even more. I'd like to address that emotion briefly here again, at the end of this powerful book, just for review.

I believe that anger can either hold us back or catapult us to making the necessary changes in our lives. As I mentioned earlier, and I am sure that you are all aware: there is a whole lot of anger floating around in the energy field on our planet right now. And it seems to be growing out of the emotion of fear. There are millions of global citizens that have a great fear for their safety, a fear of not being able to support our families and so much more. And, as many of you know, feeling safe is a main ingredient in moving from victim to victor in your life. Yet, a whole lot of us are still stuck in anger about our life situations. Let's move past that together.

Moving Beyond Fear and Anger

In fact, unless you have locked yourself in a room with no media coverage or communication with the outside world, it is impossible on this planet, in this day of great unrest for humankind, not to have been touched by fear or have it arise on some level, and, as a result, often experience emotions such as anger. As the founder of HeartMath, Doc Childre stated "a lot of us are experiencing extra stress due to the cascading effects of the financial meltdown, natural disasters, the ongoing wars, or for *any reason* through these rapidly changing times."

I believe that we have to accept this fact, and, more importantly, learn to deal with it. From my perspective, unless you can learn to master the art of controlling these emotions, you will be lacking peace—this is for sure. I further suggest that it is a time investment, well worth it. Otherwise, we'll all continue to be living in a world full of addictions by eating it away, drinking or drugging it away, going to your doctor to be fed a pill that will numb it away, or one of the other alternatives that seems to be ever so popular. May I add here that through my observation, and that of many other light workers, the feeling of powerlessness causes people to want to control their environment as well. If they can't find power or peace within, they tend to attempt to take others' power away. I like the first alternative. Learning to feel it, accept it, and then allow it to move through you and attempt to feel at peace once again, as best that you can. That is the essence of learning self-empowerment and leaving the victim mindset behind.

> *Between stimulus and response, there is a space. In that space*
> *lies our freedom and power to choose our response. In our*
> *response lies our growth and freedom.*
> —Victor Frankl, *Man's Search for Meaning*

Things to Know About Anger

Anger is a powerful emotion. It can be used either in productive or counterproductive ways. It is like electricity. It can be beneficial, such as operating your entire household with ease—providing heat, light, and entertainment; or, if not used properly, it can electrocute you.

It is a powerful survival tool, but remember, when we are angry, our brain often downshifts to a lower evolutionary level and can wreak havoc on our health when stored up in our bodies for a prolonged period of time. What if you continue to repress it? It will end up damaging your body, mind, and spirit! Harness it, and learn to use it for the highest good of all. Think of the example of using a teapot to create the perfect temperature water to steep your favorite flavor of tea: If you turn the temperature down, and allow the steam to release when the whistle begins to blow, rather than letting it boil and create an unpleasant explosion. The result can be a perfect temperature of water to make a delightful cup of tea. Learn to effectively take control your God-given emotional system embedded in your human psyche, and you can choose to use it to fuel your natural gifts, talents, and personal passions to help mankind. Nature has developed the emotional state we call "anger" to help us stay alive. Anger sends signals to all parts of our body to help us fight or flee. It energizes us to prepare us for action. Many years ago, wild animals that wanted to eat us threatened us. Now we more often feel threatened by other human beings, either psychologically or physically. Again, watch the nightly news for evidence of this reality.

Yet we can choose to feel energized by anger. We can ask ourselves how to put this energy to the most productive use. That way, you won't pollute your body's health.

What I have learned to do is to harness anger to empower myself, and so have many of my co-authors. These authors reflect in their stories and, by their actions in creating their Facebook posts, have consciously chosen at this point in our lives, to allow ourselves to use this emotion of anger, to fuel our passion to make a difference, in our own lives, and that of others.

I have plenty of challenges, just like anyone else in my life, in fact, maybe a few more than the average person. I've lived life hard. I've worked hard, played hard, and definitely learned my lessons the hard way. I've lived through childhood incest, a violent date rape in college, more sexual assaults, and was stalked for nine years by someone that the police never did reveal to me and would you believe more?. I suffered with childhood obesity, adolescent depression, and was the youngest of six children while growing up in the 1960s and 70s. I started working for the public library system at 14 years of age. By the time I was a teenager, my father had become a successful entrepreneur and I was considered spoiled by my older siblings. This fact is something that they have never have quite forgiven me for to this day, as my four eldest siblings grew up in poverty during much of their childhood. By the time I was a teenager, my father had made it as a middle class successful entrepreneur. The result was that he had it to share with his children that were still living at home, and being that I was the baby of the family, I benefited the most.

Now, I also went through domestic abuse in relationships, and the list of results from my living in the victim mindset could go on and on.

I also was in four auto accidents, and suffered a head trauma and neck injury while working for an airline, not long after my dream came true to have my first book published by an American publishing house. Let's just say that I've self-titled myself to be a former "queen of the victim mindset." And for a good reason, as I've seen violence, experienced violence, and still have PTSD symptoms, if you need a label for it, from many traumatic experiences.

I can authentically tell you that I am one of the 99 percent that Occupy Wall Street had organized themselves to defend. I've been homeless—hell, I had to house myself—only by the grace of friends letting me live with them. four times when I was living in the thick of victimhood. And, there was yet another time in my life experience, when, after being hurt at work, and having workmen's compensation deny my revised claim, when I didn't know if I would have a place to live at all. As a result of the brain injury, I went through speech therapy just to be able to put sentences together properly again and not continually repeat myself. And, as for the continuous and excruciating headaches that ensued after that injury? Well, once a chiropractor, with specialized training in cranial sacral techniques, was successfully helping me to overcome them. The insurance company decided that they wouldn't pay for the treatment. My alternative? Megadoses of pharmaceutical pain medications. Again, I've written more about that in my next book.

I've also struggled to feed my children as a single parent, gone to food shelves to do just that, and *allowed* their father to run me emotionally into the ground. More recently, I stood by feeling helpless as my elderly parents were asked to fill out their refinancing documents a total of nineteen times, in order to attempt to save their house that they have lived in for forty-four years! I just spoke with my mother last night and she said that they might have hope! Can you believe it? This same bank (one that has been in the news an awful lot for just this type of scandal, and received a huge bailout by the U.S. government) just responded to their attorney. And, guess what? Now, they are allowing them to fill it out one more time! Yes, this is a true fact; they get to fill out those refinancing documents out for the *twentieth time*! And, that has given my 78-year-old mother hope. Are you with me here? I am practicing my anger management techniques as I share this story with you.

Mind you, without my mother's enormous amount of faith in God, I am sure that this whole situation would have about driven her mad! As for the documents being filled out twenty times: If you think that I am kidding, well, you fact checkers, I can give you proof, if you want it. Enough about my story, let's move forward.

> *The global community is being called on to shift from the*
> *pursuit of self-gain at the expense of others—to a more*
> *balanced system of care for the rights and needs of the people.*
> —from Doc Childre, founder of HeartMath®

We Are the Ones that We've Been Waiting For

Okay, I have a dream. I have a burning desire and passion in my belly that still believes in mankind. I have a thread of hope in my brothers and sisters, that we all come together to create the tipping point that will change our present reality. I believe that we can still rise up together, and change this dismal reality that we as mankind have participated in creating, a reality that we are existing in right now that had to get this bad for us all to have no choice *but* to see it.

> *When you get lost in the dream,*
> *you forget you are the dreamer.*
> —Lori Rekowski

You see, we as human beings know innately, as I mentioned earlier in this story, that no man is an island. Underneath it all, we inherently know that we are all connected at some level. Physicists have actually proved this to be the case in modern history. I've come to the conclusion after years of study that we, simply by being born as human beings, want to help others that have been through tragedies similar to ours. Media coverage of natural disasters tell tales of this reality over and over throughout time.

I also believe that we humans are remarkably resilient and capable of doing the unthinkable. How many of us have witnessed our sisters and brothers go through unspeakable tragedies, such as the loss of a child, or violent attacks, murders of loved ones, or kidnappings, and then watched or read stories about these men and women, as they healed themselves? They healed themselves time after time, survivor after survivor, by dedicating their lives to helping others to recover from the same thing that they had gone through. Or better yet? They created a movement to *prevent* those tragedies from happening to others.

As I close on our journey together in this book, I end with yet another song that has often kept me going when I temporarily lost faith.

> *The longer I live the more I believe*
> *You do have to give if you wanna receive*
> *There's a time to listen, a time to talk*
> *And you might have to crawl even after you walk*
> *Had sure things blow up in my face*
> *Seen the long shot, win the race*
> *Been knocked down by the slamming door*
> *Picked myself up and came back for more*
> —*Life's a Dance*, by John Michael Montgomery

Thank you for sharing in our vision. Come and join us on Facebook or at our websites. We'd love for you to be a part of our team. I'll meet you back here for the last volume of this behind the scenes journey, due out in 2013.

With love and respect,

Lori Rekowski, *A Victim No More*

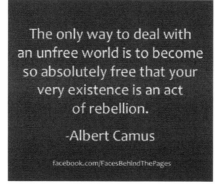